C000285969

Foreign Assistance of Illiberal and Autocratic Regimes

Sevinç Öztürk

Foreign Assistance of Illiberal and Autocratic Regimes

PETER LANG

Lausanne • Berlin • Bruxelles • Chennai • New York • Oxford

Library of Congress Cataloging-in-Publication Data
A CIP catalog record for this book has been applied for at the
Library of Congress.

Bibliographic information published by the Deutsche Nationalbibliothek.
The German National Library lists this publication in the German National
Bibliography; detailed bibliographic data is available on the Internet
at http://dnb.d-nb.de.

ISBN 978-3-631-88541-3 (Print)
E-ISBN 978-3-631-90407-7 (E-PDF)
E-ISBN 978-3-631-90408-4 (E-PUB)
10.3726/b20948

© 2023 Peter Lang Group AG, Lausanne
Published by Peter Lang GmbH, Berlin, Deutschland

info@peterlang.com - www.peterlang.com

All rights reserved.
All parts of this publication are protected by copyright.
Any utilisation outside the strict limits of the copyright law, without the
permission of the publisher, is forbidden and liable to prosecution.
This applies in particular to reproductions, translations, microfilming,
and storage and processing in electronic retrieval systems.

This publication has been peer reviewed.

Abstract: Research on the relationship between regime type and foreign aid allocation is limited in theoretical explanations and empirical support. This research attempts to fill this gap by aiming to find out why autocratic and illiberal states give foreign aid, recognizing that aid provision is not peculiar to liberal democracies. This study suggests a distinct theoretical mechanism for the assistance of non-democratic countries. I argue that, in non-democratic and illiberal countries, the nature of the relationship between the leader and business elites affects the aid allocation in terms of motivation and preferences over aid policies. Countries with illiberal and autocratic regimes become donors due to the political influence of business elites, given that foreign aid policies benefit business elites, particularly those that are politically influential. Concurrently, in these countries, business-elite configuration influences the preferences of aid allocation. Using data from Enterprise Survey, OECD, and AidData, this study employs quantitative analysis and finds that non-democratic and illiberal regimes with high influence from the business elites are more likely to provide aid in much higher amounts. Besides, using data from the World Bank and AidData, the findings of quantitative analyses show that the dominance in the business-elite structure drives the leaders to provide higher-value aid projects to the nations in need with less variation in the aid sector. Robustness checks are implemented with alternative tests.

Keywords: Foreign Aid, Non-democratic Donors, Politically Connected Firms, Illiberal Donors, Aid Preferences

Dedicated to my lovely daughter, Naz.

Author's Note

This book is derived from the Ph.D. dissertation titled "Foreign Aid Allocation by Autocratic and Illiberal Regimes: Influence and Competition of Business Elites," completed at Rutgers, the State University of New Jersey in 2019.

Acknowledgment

I would like to express my gratitude to my adviser, Prof. Manus I. Midlarsky for his continued support and immense knowledge. I also would like to thank Dr. Andrey Tomashevskiy, Dr. Xian Huang, and Dr. Esra Çeviker Gürakar for their support, encouragement, and inspiration during the study of my Ph.D. dissertation.

Contents

List of Figures

List of Tables

Chapter 1 Introduction

Abstract: Recent decades have witnessed the emergence and rise of foreign aid donors with illiberal or non-democratic regimes. This book aims to discover why these countries have emerged as foreign aid donors. To examine this question, this chapter formulates the research questions raised throughout the book with the background of these questions. The chapter discusses why examining the assistance of non-democratic and illiberal donors from the domestic political perspective is significant. Briefly, this chapter provides an overview of the book.

Keywords: Emerging Donors, Non-DAC donors, Non-democratic Donors, Illiberal Donors, Domestic Politics of Aid

1.1. Introduction

In October 2017, Hun Sen,[1] the Prime Minister of Cambodia, implied that Cambodia is choosing China over the United States by challenging the US to cut the U.S. foreign aid; Cambodia also signed a foreign aid agreement with China (Thul, 2017, 2018). Chinese influence in Cambodia is not new; China has been providing foreign aid to Cambodia since 1956[2] (Marsot, 1969); however, this event clearly shows that in comparison to the U.S. aid, China has increased its influence on Cambodia as becoming the top donor in this country.

This is not the only case where Chinese foreign aid takes over the influence of U.S. foreign aid. According to data released by AidData (AidData, 2017b),[3] a research lab at the College of William and Mary, China has become a global provider of foreign aid. Samantha Custer, director of policy analysis at AidData, stated that "If the U.S. follows through on its rhetoric and scales back its global footprint, China may be well-positioned to step into the breach and cement its role as a preferred donor and lender to the developing world" (Griffiths, 2017). Figure 1.1 illustrates the Chinese foreign assistance since the 1990s.[4]

---

1 Full name of the Prime Minister of Cambodia is Samdech Akka Moha Sena Padei Techo Hun Sen.
2 China began to provide foreign aid in 1950s; however, China has dropped the amount of aid and even stopped it for a period between 1970s and 1990s.
3 For more information about the Chinese foreign aid: http://china.aiddata.org/.
4 OECD has two different data for Chinese foreign aid. One of them is on the aid of Chinese Taipei, and the other one is based on the OECD estimates from People's

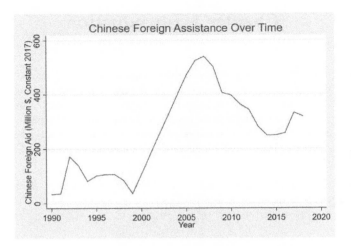

Figure 1.1. Chinese Foreign Assistance Since the 1990s

Although Chinese foreign assistance is one of the most notable cases that attracted scholarly attention, the assistance of non-democratic countries in the international foreign aid regime and the legitimacy of their aid have also been discussed beyond the Chinese example. Venezuela's aid package to Cuba and Nicaragua to transfer its model to these countries, Iran's aid to Lebanon to prove itself as a regional power, and Russia's foreign assistance to Nicaragua as the largest Russian aid recipient, have largely been debated and sometimes criticized in the media and academic studies (Asmus, Fuchs, & Muller, 2018; Naim, 2009; Woods, 2008).[5]

Why did China suddenly emerge as a major aid provider? Why is one of the largest aid recipients of Russia a small Central American country, Nicaragua, which is highly far away from Russia (Asmus et al., 2018)? How does Turkey turn into one of the largest foreign aid providers despite being a middle-income country with its recent history as an aid recipient? Why does Saudi Arabia grow

---

Republic of China. Figure 1.1 used the Chinese Taipei data. To see the Chinese aid based on the second data, see Figure A.1.

5   Naim (2009) has called the assistance from non-democratic countries as "rouge aid." Following Naim (2009), scholars have been analyzing if aid of non-democracies such as China is, indeed, different than the traditional donors such as the US (Dreher et al., 2011).

to help other nations for development as one of the top donors, in defiance of its pessimistic history with empowerment rights and women's rights (Cingranelli, Richards, & Clay, 2014)?[6] Why would these countries provide aid, although their regimes do not possess the liberal characteristics of democracy, given that foreign aid donation is traditionally considered to be a task peculiar to liberal countries?

A straightforward answer could be that each of these countries aims to be more powerful and influential in international politics, either globally or regionally, and foreign aid is a tool for achieving this goal. Aid for influence has been discussed since the emergence of aid practices in international politics.[7] Indeed, studies[8] show that countries provide aid in order to be more influential on the recipient nation or region and in the international arena. In parallel with its increasing foreign assistance, China's growing influence on African countries is a concrete example of this argument (Shinn, 2019).

While aid for influence can be used to explain the international motivations of these donors, it does not capture the entire story behind aid giving. Aid for influence implies the aid provision to other nations for receiving policy concessions by altering the policies of the recipient government in exchange for the aid. Yet, these policy concessions can vary for different countries. Russia, for instance, might be pursuing different policy concessions compared to the United States. Additionally, the beneficiaries of these policy concessions might differ.

Moreover, aid for influence refers to the international aspect of aid giving, but the domestic aspect is missing in this explanation. To be more precise, when aid is given to other nations, this preference comes with certain consequences. With this preference, countries channel their domestic resources to other nations. When governments distribute their resources to other nations instead of spending them for the public, they risk both the budget of the nation and the support of the public. Thus, the aid policies must not be only furthered for international purposes but must also allow for domestic gains.

In this context, how can we explain the donors' domestic motivations that account for the domestic gains? An explanation regarding the domestic

---

6   The data for Saudi Arabia's violation in human rights can be found in Human Rights data by Cingranelli et al. (2014).

7   The debates on the intentions of giving aid has long history that dates back to the study of Morgenthau (1962).

8   See Apodaca, 2017; Bearce & Tirone, 2010; Browne, 2012; Kuziemko & Werker, 2006; Lai & Morey, 2006; Morgenthau, 1962; Nelson, 1968; Nye, 1990; Rai, 1980; Smith, 2014; Wang, 1999; Wittkopf, 1973; Woods, 2008; Wright, 2009; Yuichi Kono & Montinola, 2009.

motivations of donors can be an altruistic and/or ideological explanation. These countries might be providing foreign aid because of the fundamental elements of their ideology, such as producing liberal policies and promoting liberal values such as justice, equality, and liberty. Studies find that liberal governments and liberal democratic countries are more likely to provide foreign assistance (Tingley, 2010). However, donors in examples such as Russia and Saudi Arabia cannot be explained through these liberal ideologies. Then, what other domestic factors can motivate these countries with illiberal and non-democratic regime types for aid giving? How do these factors affect their preferences on aid policies?

Another convincing perspective that may answer these questions can be that specific influential domestic actors utilize from foreign assistance in non-democratic or illiberal countries. I argue that given the potential benefit aid can provide to the business sector, politically influential business elites might be critical actors in aid policies in these countries. The primary aim of this book is to answer the above questions and understand the domestic motivations of these countries with illiberal or non-democratic regime types in their aid provision, analyzing the impact of the business elite.

1.2. Why Study the Motivations of Non-democratic and Illiberal Donors?

As the number of countries providing foreign aid has increased rapidly in international politics since the modern foreign aid giving begun with the Truman Doctrine in 1947, the debate about the effectiveness, motivations, and legitimacy of foreign aid have become more heated. Though none of the donors has stopped giving foreign assistance since then, many countries have begun to provide assistance even if they have been only recipients before (Riddell, 2007). This proliferation in the number of donors is also reflected in the different characteristics of the donors. While the established (or traditional) donors have democratic and liberal characteristics, the new donors show varieties in terms of their regime types (see Figure 1.2).

Figure 1.2. Foreign Aid Donors Between 2013 and 2017 Based on Regime Classification[9]

9   Countries in white are not donors between the years of 2013 and 2017. Regimes are identified based on V- Dem's regime- type variable (v2x_ regime) (Coppedge et al., 2018a; Pemstein et al., 2019).

These donors with different regime types are listed in the classification of The Organization for Economic Cooperation and Development (OECD) as non-members of the Development Assistance Committee (DAC or non-DAC). Even though the massive amount of foreign assistance in the world is still coming from the DAC members, which are also liberal democracies, according to the OECD's data on development flow, the non-DAC countries provided 23.7 billion dollars in 2019 (OECD, 2023). Moreover, some of these countries have even become the most prominent donors. OECD's reports (2019b) present the top 30 donor countries, and eight of these countries are non-democratic or illiberal donors. Besides, among these donors, countries such as Turkey and Qatar are more generous than some of the traditional liberal democratic donors such as France, Japan, and the US (see Figure 1.3).

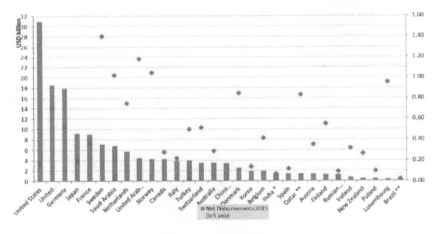

Figure 1.3. Largest Thirty Donors According to the OECD[10,11]

Despite the increased number of donors and amount of foreign aid in the international arena, there is little systematic analysis of the domestic motivations of all non-democratic donors. The question of domestic motives of non-democratic donors lacks both generalizable theoretical background and empirical support. While the literature on the motivations of donors relies mostly on complex interdependence theory for the international motivations of donors, it rarely considers domestic factors. Moreover, the research about the internal motives of non-democratic donors is mainly limited to the China case and rarely goes beyond it. Even if some empirical case studies exist about the other non-democratic donors, they either analyze non-democratic donors with the same theoretical framework as traditional liberal democratic donors or analyze only one case, which hinders generalizations.

However, the non-democratic donors are different from the traditional donors with regard to the size of their economy, the level of corruption and favoritism, human rights violation, their experience in aid giving, their international status, their historical background, and their region. The foreign policy behavior of the countries is based not only on the states' behavior as a unitary actor but also on the interactions of the within-state factors. Therefore, while there are so many differences regarding their domestic politics and size in the economy, it might not be proper to expect the same motivation from non-democratic donors as anticipated from traditional liberal democratic donors.

The consideration of the internal motivations of non-democratic donors in international politics is essential for at least two main reasons. First, though it still does not represent the majority amount, non-democratic donors are providing a significant amount of aid to other countries. In 2015, they, together, provided 18 billion dollars[12] in 2015. This amount does not even include the exact amount of some of the non-democratic or illiberal donors, such as Brazil or Qatar, because some of these donors still do not report their foreign aid policies to the OECD. Besides, this amount might even increase in the future.[13]

Due to the increased number of donors and the increased amount and share of foreign aid provided by non-DAC members or emerging donors in general, foreign aid became a more significant foreign policy tool in international politics. A higher number of donors leads to a higher number of options for the recipient countries. When the recipients have more options, the other donors have

---

12 I calculated the total amount of these countries by selecting the donor countries which score lower than 3 on V-Dem's regime-type variable (v2x_reg) and using the aid data from OECD foreign aid for these countries.

13 The amount of Brazil and Qatar's assistance have been used as estimates from the OECD's report.

become less influential over the recipient; therefore, donors have more conflict due to overlapping agendas over foreign aid. Hence, the foreign assistance of new donors is not usually welcome by most traditional donors, particularly when given by non-democratic or illiberal countries. Given the importance of these new donors as game changers in international politics, understanding their domestic motivations related to this soft power foreign policy tool is essential. Understanding the motivations of these donors can inform both the traditional donors and recipients and shape the perception of these donors.

Second, foreign aid, as a foreign policy tool, involves many actors, from the initiation of the policy to the construction or delivery of goods and services. Therefore, many state actors, as well as within-state and non-state actors, are involved in this process. Without fully accounting for the importance of these factors in the foreign aid policy decision-making process, foreign aid literature will be limited. Examining the within-state factors that involve the causal mechanism of this foreign policy tool will provide us with a more comprehensive theoretical picture about the states' soft power foreign policy decision-making. Related to that, looking at the spillover effect of aid giving for domestic and non-state actors in a country interestingly shows economic mobilization. For instance, DEIK[14] in Turkey regulates Turkish investments abroad and is closely related to this aid-giving process in Turkey.

With all these in mind, this book aims to construct an empirically supported theoretical explanation of domestic motivations of donor countries with illiberal and non-democratic regimes, utilizing but not being limited to the main assertions of Selectorate Theory (De Mesquita & Smith, 2007, 2009, 2012; De Mesquita, Smith, Siverson, & Morrow, 2004). For a theory of domestic motivations of emerging donors, it is essential to understand the patterns, dynamics, and interactions between the factors within the non-democratic and illiberal donors. This descriptive understanding helps us to construct a theory and will fill a substantial gap in our exploration of the motivations of various donors. Thus, I ask what domestic political and economic variables explain the aid provision in donor countries with autocratic or illiberal regimes. Why do leaders in non-democratic donors provide foreign aid? To answer these questions, I develop a theory of foreign assistance in autocratic and illiberal regimes by analyzing the influence of business elites on the motivation and preferences over aid policies.

Furthermore, to be able to answer this broader question above and test the theory, this research seeks to answer the secondary questions below:

---

14   Foreign Economic Relations Board of Turkey.

- What is the relationship between regime type and foreign aid policies of autocratic donors? How does the regime type of autocratic donors influence the motivation of their foreign aid? What kind of political settings do regime types create for the interaction of domestic actors on foreign aid policies in non-democratic countries? How do foreign aid policies contribute to the private goods opportunities in donor countries?
- Which actor(s) play a role in aid provision in autocratic countries, and why? What is the role of business elites in driving the leader to provide aid in non-democratic countries? What is the interaction between the business elite and the leader of the country deciding on aid policies?
- What role does elite configuration play in shaping autocratic donor governments' foreign aid policies? Does the level of competition between the business elites determine aid amount, target countries, or the type of assistance they provide?

To address these questions, I utilize a quantitative statistical approach, collecting and analyzing data that allow for a cross-national quantitative analysis of the domestic motivations of non-domestic donors both on the country-year and dyad-year levels. The following is a literature review chapter where I address previous and current literature on donors' motivations and how the theory developed in this study would fit into this literature. Chapter 3 discusses the motivation and preferences of autocratic donors by suggesting and detailing the theory and hypotheses. In chapter 4, the domestic motivation of donors is tested with quantitative methodology. Chapter 5 will continue to analyze the foreign aid of autocratic and illiberal donors in terms of their preferences. Finally, chapter 6 includes the conclusions, limitations, practical and theoretical implications, as well as suggestions for future research.

Chapter 2 Literature Review

Abstract: The literature on foreign aid motivations of donors mainly examines the motivations of donor countries with the theories of international relations. A few studies focus on the domestic motivations of donor countries, and these studies are primarily limited to DAC members as donor countries, which are liberal democratic countries. This chapter reviews the literature on the motivations of foreign aid donors in two steps. First, the literature on how donor countries use foreign aid as an instrument for foreign policy is explained. Then, the literature on the domestic motivations of donors will be discussed based on three main domestic factors: regime type, ideology, and interests.

Keywords: Foreign Aid Literature, Donor Motivation, Domestic Motivation of Donors, Regime Type of Donors

2.1. Introduction

This chapter will review the literature that addresses the motivations of donor countries and discuss how the research in this study will fit into this literature. In order to do so, first, I will review the existing literature that focuses on the international motivations of donors. Then, I will continue by addressing the studies that link domestic politics with aid policies based on three main variables: regime type, ideology, and interests.

2.2. Foreign Aid as an Instrument of Foreign Policy

Although the true motivation of donor countries is supposed to be helping out the countries in need, in real-world politics, this usually is not the case. A key aspect of the international relations field concerns "why states provide aid" as part of their foreign policy. In parallel with international relations theory, scholars of the donor states have studied donor states mainly as unitary actors and similarly focused on international and regional levels of analysis.

In general, arguments made in real-world politics and academic literature suggest that the purposes of the donor countries in aid giving can be classified into four main categories, including diplomatic, developmental, humanitarian, and commercial (Lancaster, 2008). However, given the broadness of the term diplomacy, many kinds of donor motivations can be included in this category. The objectives of providing foreign aid are: making an ally, increasing the volume of trade, protecting themselves by spreading their ideology, growing donor prestige or allies' prestige,[15] increasing economic development in the recipient, and decreasing the probability of political conflicts such as civil war, extremism, and terrorism.[16]

Theoretical approaches to the purposes of foreign aid primarily benefit from international relations theories but rarely from theories of foreign policy decision-making that discuss the impacts of domestic politics on foreign policy decisions.[17] These theories of international relations can typically be grouped under four main approaches: Realism, Idealism, Constructivism, and Marxism. In the realist international relations approach, foreign aid is considered as a foreign policy tool that has been employed since the Cold War's bipolar struggle to influence the recipient country's politics, so aid policies are driven by the strategic interests of nation-states (Hattori, 2001). The quantities, the recipients, and the types of given aid are determined by the national strategic interests, which, in return, influences aid effectiveness (Riddell, 1987). For example, one of the leading scholars of realism, Hans Morgenthau (1962), defines foreign aid as "the transfer of money, goods, and services from one nation to another" (p. 371). He identifies six different types of aid; however, he argues that all of them, except humanitarian aid, are, in fact, a bribe of the donor country to further the national strategic interests (Morgenthau, 1962).[18]

Idealists, on the other hand, have a more optimistic view on foreign aid, challenging the realists and emphasizing the importance of humanitarian and developmental purposes in aid allocation (Raposo, 2013; Riddell, 1987). According to this theoretical approach, foreign aid is "a set of programmatic measures designed to enhance the socio-economic and political development of recipient countries" (Hattori, 2001, p. 634). In this context, foreign aid, as a

---

15   By providing foreign aid, donors not only aim to be seen prestigious in the international politics, but also, they aim their allies to be seen prestigious. For example, it is argued that the purpose of the U.S. Marshall Plan was promoting the prestige of the Greece which has been an ally with the US. Morgenthau (1962) calls it as "prestige aid."

16   Simply put, donors provide aid for international security concerns.

17   Distinction has been made between theories of international relations and theories of foreign policy decision-making. The theories of international politics explain the interactions between states under the international structure that constrains states to take certain actions (Waltz, 1996). On the other hand, the theories of foreign policy explain the behavior of the states which are in the same system, but act differently (Waltz, 1996). Also, theories of international politics focus on the systemic analysis while theories of foreign policy make domestic explanations (Waltz, 1996).

18   Morgenthau (1962) elucidates that even humanitarian assistance can be a bribe under certain circumstances.

soft power[19] resource, can increase the interdependence between countries and even beyond that between international organizations and countries. However, this idea has some similarities with the realist approach, particularly in the levels of analysis and explanations regarding the purposes of aid. More specifically, the theory of complex interdependence still applies to nation-states and considers the purpose of giving foreign aid as generating influence in the recipient state.

Marxist theories approach foreign aid as a tool of capital elites. When this applies to international politics, foreign aid is considered as a tool of dominant capitalist states to influence and exploit developing countries (Lancaster, 2008). For example, in world systems theory,[20] foreign aid, as a means of constraining the development path of recipient countries, promotes the unequal accumulation of capital in the world. It expands the gap between industrial and developing countries, increasing the inequality between the nations (Veltmeyer & Metras, 2005).

Constructivist scholars have a different take on the definition of foreign aid. Hattori (2001), for instance, defines foreign aid as "the symbolic power politics between donor and recipient," interpreting it based on "norms" and "values." However, like Marxist scholars, they focus on the importance of material hierarchy between the giver and receiver. Accordingly, "aid practice transfers material dominance and subordination into gestures of generosity and gratitude. This symbolic transformation, in turn, euphemizes the material hierarchy underlying the donor-recipient relation" (Hattori, 2001, p. 639). In this complicity, recipients adopt the recipient role, give their social power to the donor, follow the order that prioritizes the donors, and subordinate the recipient in the social hierarchy.

Based on these theoretical approaches, empirical research has sought to identify the various national motivations of donor countries and measured the influence of these countries on national, regional, and/or international politics. The broad academic consensus suggests that donor countries provide foreign aid for strategic reasons, referring to the realist paradigm. Only a few researches that include cases from Nordic countries such as Norway and Sweden suggest that these cases deviate from the broad approach because these countries provide

---

19   Nye (1990) coined the term of soft power.
20   World System Theory is developed by Immanuel Wallerstein. For more information about the historical progress of distribution of wealth between core, semi-peripheral and peripheral countries, see Wallerstein (1974).

aid for humanitarian reasons and poverty reduction (Alesina & Dollar, 2000; Omoruyi, 2017), which is more explanatory in the idealist/liberal paradigm.

In one of the most significant studies about the determinants of foreign aid in donor countries, Alesina and Dollar (2000) have found that, in general, foreign aid policies are driven by political and strategic considerations as much as by the economic needs and policy performance of the recipients. The target of the Nordic countries (Norway, Sweden, and Finland) is mainly developing countries, which seems to be verifying that these countries are providing aid for poverty reduction. On the other hand, the largest three donors—Japan, US, and France—have different pathways: the U.S. targets about one-third of its total assistance to Egypt and Israel, while France prefers to provide aid to its former colonies, and Japan gives it to its UN friends. When the recipient countries of the US are not Israel and Egypt, the U.S. foreign aid is provided for reducing poverty and spreading democracy and openness (Alesina & Dollar, 2000).

Although Schraeder, Hook, and Taylor (1998) reached similar conclusions regarding the strategic considerations of aid, they disagree that Nordic countries provide assistance for altruistic and humanitarian purposes. Using cross-national time-series analysis, the authors tested six different motivations of donor countries: humanitarian need, strategic importance, economic potential, cultural similarity, ideological stance, and region. They found that while strategic and ideological interests drive the US to give aid, Japan gives aid for economic benefits (apolitical nature). Besides, Sweden gives aid mostly to Southern African countries for ideological purposes, whereas France gives aid to countries that show cultural similarities with France (Schraeder, Hook, & Taylor, 1998). Moreover, in analyzing the US as a case, Lancaster (2008) concluded with a similar argument about the motivations of U.S. aid. Lancaster (2008) also argues that U.S. foreign aid is used to pursue a variety of national purposes, including providing humanitarian relief, furthering diplomatic goals, promoting development and democracy abroad, addressing global issues, supporting economic and political transitions, expanding export markets, preventing and mitigating conflict, and strengthening weak states.

Not only the empirical literature on the cases of traditional donors shares the conventional view that foreign aid is given for political, economic, and strategic considerations, but also empirical research on the new donors concluded that the new donors have strategic and political interests in foreign aid giving. Naim (2009) pointed out the aid of these new donors as "rouge aid," arguing that these new donors with non-democratic regimes are trying to transfer their own political regimes to their recipients. In that sense, for example, Chinese foreign aid has been especially discussed in the literature. Scholars have argued that Chinese aid is driven by its ideological, economic, strategic, and political interests (Brautigam, 2009; Li, 2009).

Accordingly, China is mainly providing foreign aid to Asian and African countries; in return, the Chinese government is spreading its ideology to the recipient countries and increasing trade volume with them. Indeed, China has become the most prominent new investor, trader, buyer, and aid donor in many African countries (Brautigam, 2009). In response to these critics, in their quantitative study, Dreher and Fuchs (2015) have analyzed China's donor motivation, as it is one of the non-democratic donors, and have drawn a different picture, using Chinese project aid data that covers between 1956 and 2006. Creating a dataset from China's aid projects, they (Dreher & Fuchs, 2015) make a counterargument that Chinese aid cannot be considered as rouge aid because China does not pay significantly more attention to politics compared to traditional donors, even though political considerations are important determinants of China's aid allocation.

Substantial work has been done to nuance the understanding of donors' motivations, even including the countries that have started to provide aid in the last decade. Though each of these theoretical approaches explains foreign aid from different perspectives, they all share some similar characteristics. More specifically, they all look for the motivations of aid in the international area and analyze the motivations as if foreign aid decisions are sourcing from unitary states without taking into consideration the policy-making processes. Empirical evidence supported these theories without unpacking the states (and their policies) into smaller units and examining the effects of these units on the donors' foreign aid decisions.

However, by focusing on donors' international and regional motivations and taking the nation-state as a unitary actor, we ignore the importance of domestic factors in the foreign aid decision-making process. That is, in addition to the new donors[21] entering foreign aid politics and being able to take their place in the global economic development arena, their domestic politics can also be a driving force. I seek to contribute to the existing literature on foreign policy decision-making literature by broadening the idea of "bringing the domestic politics" in foreign aid policies and discussing the potential impacts of domestic politics, specifically business elites, on the foreign aid policies of donors.

---

21   New donors consist of all non-democratic and illiberal donors.

2.3. Shifting Focus to the Domestic Motivations of Donors

Discussions on donor motivations often consider how foreign aid is allocated and why it is so. This question that there needs to be a domestic political process before these policies are implemented begins with Ruttan (1996). Ruttan (1996) argues that a mix of internal economic, political, intellectual, and cultural factors led to the change in U.S. development policy between the 1940s and 1990s. Verifying the impact of the Vietnam War and other external factors on aid policy, Ruttan (1996) also successfully shows that aid policies are determined by a mix of domestic constituencies, including those between and within the executive and legislative branches. Inspired by and expanding on Ruttan's study (1996), Lancaster (2008) continues this inquiry and writes meticulously about the impacts and dynamics of domestic politics on foreign aid policies, identifying the importance of ideas, institutions, organizations, and interest groups. To support her argument, she has done an in-depth case study analysis covering five countries—the US, Japan, France, Germany, and Denmark and examined how domestic pressures from the different state organizations affected foreign aid policies (Lancaster, 2008). Below, I will detail the literature that focuses specifically on institutions, ideas, and interests as the motive for donors.

2.3.1. Institutional Explanations: Democracies vs. Non-Democracies

While Lancaster (2008)'s study is one of the most influential research which offers an in-depth analysis of the domestic politics of foreign aid, as she also noted, her study is not based on a consistent theoretical explanation. On the other hand, De Mesquita and Smith (2007, 2009) apply the Selectorate Theory of foreign policy to foreign aid motivations of donor countries to examine the impact of regime type on the foreign aid motivations of the leaders. Deriving their hypothesis based on the assumption that all leaders would like to ensure their political survival, De Mesquita and Smith (2009) argue that foreign aid is one of the tools that leaders use to enhance their term in power. To them (De Mesquita & Smith, 2007, 2009), leaders' foreign aid policies differ in small winning coalition-size governments (autocracies or rigged electoral regimes) and large winning coalition-size governments (democracies). De Mesquita and Smith (2007, 2009) argue that all leaders want to survive; therefore, they need to provide public or private goods for their supporters. In large winning coalition systems, the selectorates would like to obtain some policy concessions from the recipient countries that can be transformed into public goods. However, in small winning coalition-size governments, the supporters of the leader are not the voters, but the leaders' survival depends on the support of political and economic elites.

Therefore, in those systems, leaders provide aid to gain some policy concession that can be transformed into private goods which can benefit the political and economic elites. De Mesquita and Smith's (2009) departure point that leaders would like to survive politically is valid; however, their empirical tests do not include autocratic countries. They (De Mesquita & Smith, 2009) find that leaders in large winning coalition-size systems are more likely to provide foreign aid than small coalition-size governments by testing only DAC countries with large winning coalition systems, in other words, liberal democracies. On the other hand, looking at the new donors, one can observe that regime type of donors shows high variations, including democratic (large winning coalition) countries.

Focusing on the democratic states, Annen and Strickland's study (2017) emphasizes the role of elections as another institutional explanation. Accordingly, once they are in power, governments need to keep their promises since the public cares about how they act. Because voters cannot observe all the government spending, humanitarian assistance is one visible way to show their expenditure. Analyzing the DAC donors, Annen and Strickland (2017) find that governments increase their humanitarian aid spending by 19 percent one year before the election. However, Annen and Strickland (2017) also do not include non-DAC members or non-democracies in their analysis.

2.3.2. Ideological Explanations

Research on foreign policy decision-making consistently considers that political ideology of the leader and incumbent party to be a key determinant of their foreign policies. Accordingly, ideology determines whether governments or leaders will seek hawkish or dovish politics, use soft power or hard power tools, or seek strategic or humanitarian and distributive justice purposes (Haas, 2003; Narizny, 2003). This consideration is also reflected in the foreign aid policies of states. Theories that attempt to explain the domestic origins of aid are not limited to bureaucratic and institutional explanations; they also account for the ideological factor. Based on the domestic explanation of foreign aid policies, leftist parties, religious organizations, and relief agencies are determinants of these policies (Lumsdaine, 1987).

The empirical support of this explanation comes from Tingley's cross-national time-series analysis (Tingley, 2010). Using data from OECD foreign aid dataset, Tingley (2010) finds that "as governments become more conservative, their aid effort is likely to fall." Tingley (2010) further argues that "domestic political variables appear to influence aid effort, but only for aid to low-income countries and multilaterals while aid effort to middle-income countries is unaffected" (p. 41). However, one limitation to the generalizability of his study is that Tingley (2010) does not include all the donor countries in his study. Instead, he (Tingley, 2010) analyzes only DAC donor countries' foreign aid. That means the research may or may not apply to the non-DAC donor countries, which have different domestic mechanisms with respect to their regime types, smaller size economies, and smaller status in international relations.

The impact of the government ideology, culture, and/ or belief has been studied beyond the DAC countries, even though there are few studies yet. One study that refers to the importance of ideology and belief beyond the liberal governments is on Turkish foreign assistance. Kavakli (2018) shows that government ideology matters in aid policies using the Turkish case. According to his findings, while Turkish aid was given for international alignments and coethnicity before the AKP[22] government, it has been targeted more to Muslim nations as economic and humanitarian assistance with the AKP government. However, Kavakli (2018) does not generalize his study to non-democratic countries but to emerging donors in general.

Therefore, this study seeks to fill this gap in the theoretical explanation of non-democratic donors and contribute to the literature on the domestic motivations of donors by measuring this relationship in the non-democratic and illiberal donor countries. Studying it beyond the democratic donors, including all non-democratic and illiberal donors in the analysis, will enhance the generalizability of the theory.

2.3.3. Interests-based Explanations: Accounting the Business in

Interest groups such as firms, manufacturers, and NGOs in the foreign aid decision-making process have also been highlighted as the actors that drive the donors to distribute foreign aid because once public resources are involved in the process, they become a dynamic force in economic actors as well. For example, Diven (2001), using a time-series quantitative research design, analyzes the relationship between commodity producers' interests and the amount of U.S. food aid and finds that large grain stocks correlated with the higher levels of food aid in the following year of aid. Moreover, commercial exports are negatively correlated to food aid shipments, which shows that food is given when the goods cannot be exported. In addition, the research (Diven, 2001) indicates that per

---

22   Adalet ve Kalkınma Partisi (Justice and Development Party).

capita, grain production in the recipient country is positively associated with total food aid shipments, proving that food aid is not targeted to the countries in need. Overall, U.S. food aid is not need-based but serves manufacturers' interests (Diven, 2001). Kim (2016) also examines the domestic politics of South Korea's foreign aid policy and reaches a similar conclusion. According to Kim (2016), while the institutional characteristics and strategic interests of the government are important in South Korea's aid policy, non-government stakeholders are also critical factors for the foreign aid regime.

Although most of the studies on the economic actors of donors as the domestic driver for foreign aid have focused on case studies, commonly focusing on the US, UK, and Japan cases, the emerging literature is focusing on the new donors.[23] For instance, Breslin (2013) argues that a single actor does not determine China's relations with developing countries; corporate interests are also vital. Chinese companies can sometimes direct Chinese policy in a different direction, and developing countries can gain from China if they are not directly competing with Chinese companies.

Moreover, adding the donor's population and interest groups into the variables, Lundsgaarde (2013) hypothesized that "aid policies are either a natural extension of underlying characteristics of a country's population or an extension of a set of policies to compensate domestic actors from the vagaries of the markets" (p. 6). Analyzing four different traditional donors (US, France, Denmark, and Switzerland), Lundsgaarde (2013) examines how interest groups (firms, companies, and NGOs) are active in making the state's foreign aid policies.

Some of the aid for trade literature also emphasized the role of the exporters rather than approaching the state as a unitary actor. Accordingly, exporters can benefit from aid for trade, especially when aid is tied explicitly. When aid is tied, the recipient country has to use the aid to import goods and services from the donor country, and this will create trade opportunities for the exporters (Tajoli, 1999). However, tied aid has been reduced by the donor countries recently; and studies show that aid can benefit exporters even when the aid is not tied "if united aid generates goodwill for the donor in the recipient country" (Barthel, Neumayer, Nunnenkamp, & Seleya, 2014, p. 351). When the stock of goodwill increases trade opportunities, the donor exporters can benefit from it. Therefore, it can be considered that aid is given for export opportunities either by tying it or creating goodwill (Barthel et al., 2014).

---

23   New donors consist of all the non-democratic countries. There is no non-democratic donor among the traditional donors.

This book seeks to take regime type, ideology, and economic interests of economic groups seriously as driving forces of foreign aid policies and consider the ways in which three interact and cause foreign aid flow from the country. I seek to understand the conditions under which domestic politics can motivate non-democratic and illiberal donor countries while considering how regime type, ideology, and economic interests of governments interact. Such an inquiry is a much-needed contribution if we are moving toward a domestic political approach in foreign policy decision-making. Considering how institutions, ideology, and interests interact, I am not in search of an argument that puts aside the importance of international/regional explanations of foreign aid policies. Rather, this book seeks to help understand the foreign aid policy-making process comprehensively and seeks to be a complementary approach both to the approaches of international relations theories and to the approaches of democratic aid.

Chapter 3 Domestic Motivations and Preferences of Foreign Aid in Autocratic and Illiberal Donors

Abstract: Why do non-democratic and illiberal regimes provide aid? What determines their aid preferences? The foreign aid motivation and preferences of non-democratic or illiberal regimes are shaped by the nature of the relationship between business elites and government. This chapter of the book draws a theoretical framework about the impact of politically influential business elites on the aid decision and preferences of non-democratic or illiberal regimes.

Keywords: Foreign Aid Motivation, Politics of Foreign Aid, Aid Preferences, Politically Influential Business Elites

3.1. Introduction

The previous chapter reviewed the existing literature on the domestic motivations of donors with a focus on regime type as an explanatory factor. As is explained in the literature review, the current literature shows that democracies provide more foreign aid than autocratic donors. This argument in the current literature remained as a prevailing account until new donors with various regime types[24] arose. Yet, such an approach is still limited in its theory and empirical support. It fails to suggest an in-depth explanation concerning the domestic motivations of authoritarian donors but focuses primarily on the differences between democratic and autocratic aid giving. The argument that democracies provide more foreign aid than non-democracies overlooks the fact that non-democracies still have incentives to distribute economic resources abroad.

Then, why would autocratic and illiberal states choose to channel their economic resources into other nations via foreign aid policies? What are their preferences regarding their aid policies once they decide to provide foreign aid? The purpose of this book is to provide an examination of the domestic motivations and preferences that shape foreign aid policies in autocratic and illiberal countries. With this aim in mind, this chapter of the book offers a

---

24 For example, China, Saudi Arabia, Qatar, Turkey etc. These donors are not considered as liberal democracies and have different levels of institutionalizations.

theoretical framework regarding the aid policies of donors with autocratic and illiberal regimes.

This theoretical framework aims to disclose three issues: first, the interaction among domestic actors, their interests, and institutional mechanisms in which they operate; second, how this interaction develops the provision of foreign aid in autocratic and illiberal countries; third, how this interplay shapes preferences over aid policies in these countries.

In the following, I explain the theoretical argument on the aid motivation and preferences of autocratic countries. Then, I define the business elite and the configuration of the business elites. Following these definitions, I review the assumptions that base my theoretical argument on the state leaders' interests and on the role of the economy in the interactions of domestic actors. Third, I develop empirically testable hypotheses alongside the discussion on the theoretical argument concerning the interplay of domestic actors over aid policies. Ultimately, this chapter argues that foreign aid motivation and preferences lay at the intersection of different domestic variables and interactions of the different domestic actors.

3.2. Theory

Once economic resources are involved in the process of domestic politics, they become a dynamic force among the political actors. Depending on the regime type, political constraints accommodate the conflict of interests over the economic resources between the domestic actors.

In that context, foreign aid can be considered as an economic resource that has distributional consequences. These consequences affect multiple domestic actors such as state leaders, governments, the business sector, non-governmental organizations, and aid project workers in the field of the recipient country. As a result, due to its distributional consequences, foreign aid policies might operate among the interests of various political actors, regardless of the regime type of the state and the institutional settings that regime types create. However, depending on the regime type, the domestic constraints in which different political actors interact vary, and so do the configurations of the interaction between these domestic actors.[25]

---

25   For example, if there are not effective institutions in states, in other words, if there are not self-enforcing rules which prevent governments, leaders or ruling elites from being corrupt, the political elites might use their power for their own benefits rather

My main argument, in this context, is that foreign aid motivation and preferences in autocratic and illiberal countries originate from the nature of the relationship between domestic actors, particularly between the leader and business elites.[26] Furthermore, the nature of the relationship between the domestic actors determines the value of aid projects, the type of recipient country and sectoral distribution of aid provided by autocratic and illiberal donors. In that sense, I argue, a state with an illiberal or autocratic regime type in which the export-oriented domestic business elites have greater political influence is more likely to be a donor. However, once this donor provides foreign aid, the value of the aid projects, sectoral distribution of aid as well as the type of recipient are influenced by the configuration of business-elite groups in the autocratic or illiberal donor. To be more concrete, I propose a two-staged link between the influence of the business elite and foreign aid policies in countries with autocratic or illiberal regimes:

1. The high-political influence of business elites drives the autocratic or illiberal government to be a donor.
2. The configurations of business-elite groups influence the preferences of an autocratic or illiberal donor over foreign aid policies.

As is in democratic countries, the main aim of a leader in autocratic or illiberal institutional settings is staying in power or strengthening his/her current position. In order to do so, the leader creates a supporting coalition which is formed of the leader's supporters. While these supporters can be electorates in democratic regimes, the supporting coalition is formed of different types of elites in autocratic or illiberal regimes where there is either no election or where the elections are held, but the functionality and efficiency of the elections are still controversial.[27] Leaders in those regimes form a supporting coalition from the military, political, and business elites and keep these elites on their sides to make use of their support in maintaining their rule (Acemoglu and Robinson, 2006; Gandhi, 2008; Geddes, 1999; Geddes et al., 2018).

---

than the citizens. Therefore, political institutions stipulate the rules of the game between different actors (Acemoglu & Robinson, 2006; North & Weingast, 1989).

26   Notwithstanding, that does not mean international factors should be eliminated from the explanation of the donor motivation. On the contrary, I argue that although international factors influence foreign aid policies, domestic politics should not be ignored and taken into consideration.

27   Elections may serve different purposes in autocratic or illiberal regimes. See Gandhi and Okar (2009) for a detailed explanation.

Simultaneously, the members of supporting coalitions, particularly the elites, also benefit from the leaders' executive, legislative, and even judicial power in exchange for their support. While the interests of elites from the leader vary depending on the elite type, the interests of economic elites, particularly business elites, are usually centered around more liberal policies that can augment their revenues and interests. In this respect, business elites within the supporting coalition can benefit from the leader by encouraging the government to produce more liberal policies. The policies concerning international trade, foreign direct investment, and foreign assistance would be more advantageous for the business-elite groups as the policies made on behalf of incentivizing these areas can inflate the market opportunities of the business elites. In this regard, foreign aid might even become a more critical tool for autocratic and illiberal countries. It provides an opportunity not only to increase the trade between the recipient and donor but also for the business elite to be a contractor of the foreign aid project. Therefore, when the business elites have high-political influence in the country, these elites might encourage the leader to provide foreign assistance.

Once the aid is provided, autocratic and illiberal regimes that become donors with the political influence of business elites, shape their preferences based on the configuration of these business-elite groups. I examine two main forms of business-elite concentration: monopoly/dominance of one group of business elites and multiple/diversified business groups. Accordingly, I argue that autocratic and illiberal donors with dominant business-elite groups tend to provide aid projects that are high in value, concentrated in the sector, and targeted at resource-rich or higher-income countries. On the contrary, if there are multiple business groups in the autocratic donors,[28] I argue that the aid policies will focus on lower-value projects, multiple sectors, and lower-income countries.

The theoretical argument that the relationship between the leader and business elites shapes the foreign aid policies is based on three main assumptions. The first assumption is that while foreign aid is a foreign policy tool, foreign aid policy is determined by domestic politics. Related to the first assumption, the second assumption originates from the premises of the Selectorate Theory (De Mesquita & Smith, 2007, 2009). Accordingly, leaders mainly aim to survive in their rule. Driven by this aim, leaders employ various foreign policy tools, depending on the regime type that creates the institutional settings for their strategies on the maintenance of their power. My third assumption is that foreign aid policy

---

28   If there is a competition among these business groups.

is an economic, multi-purposed tool, that is not only given for national or international purposes but also for domestic purposes.

Relying on these three assumptions, I further assume that donor countries, particularly governments, mainly focus on their own political survival and use economic resources accordingly. In this context, they prioritize the foreign aid policies that can be of use to them for their survival and empowerment in the current system. The theoretical argument of this book suggests that the ways in which illiberal and autocratic countries provide aid are a function of relations between leader and business elites and the concentration of business elite groups.

In the following, I will define the business elite and configurations of business-elite groups and review the underlying assumptions that base for the theoretical explanation. Then, I explain why autocratic and illiberal states are motivated by their domestic policies in their aid provision in detail.

3.3. Defining Business Elite and Configurations of Business Elites

3.3.1. Business Elite

An elite is described as a minority group that has power over a larger group of which they are part. This group controls and disputes over the sources of power in society. The elite literature categorizes the different types of elites, including the political, ruling, military, and economic elite. While some of these categories overlap with others, the distinctions among the categories are evident.[29]

With respect to the definition of the elite, economic elites are considered to be a minority group who have economic power over a larger group of which they are a part. On the other hand, economic elites also have their sub-groups. Business elite is one of the sub-groups of economic elites. All different types of elites are defined according to their relative position to the other segments of society. Likewise, the business-elite group is also defined according to its position in the hierarchy of the economy and its members' level of income, education and prestige. Usually, the differences in their education level are reflected in their income, whereas the education and income level bring prestige to this group.

---

29   For example, political elites refer to the broader group than the ruling elite because political elites include the government as well as the opposition while ruling elite might only refer to the government. Ruling elite is the group whose members are ability to directly influence the politics. See Zuckerman (1977).

Yet, these characteristics of the business elite are not universal and diverge with respect to the regime type of the country that elites belong to. Particularly in autocratic countries, the business elite might be undergone a transformation by the leader due to the tendency of the autocratic leader to channel the state resources to his supporters. The leader might decide which groups should have economic power and translate this decision into policy.[30] As a result of this transformation, an autocratic leader might create a new business elite that might not belong to a highly educated class but is still wealthier than the other parts of society. Therefore, I define the business elite as follows: business elites are engaged in various sectors of business; they are relatively wealthier than the other segments of society, and they usually exercise much more power over public policies than the public does.

3.3.2. Business-Elite Configuration

In elite studies, configuration refers to the relative position and size of various elite circles in the constellation of power. In general, this configuration denotes the different types of elites, such as political, cultural, bureaucratic, cultural, etc. (Dogan, 2003). Since the focus of the book is business elites rather than elites in general, I apply the concept of elite configuration to the business elite by denoting the different types of business elites in economic sectors such as agricultural, industrial, manufacturing, etc. In this context, the relative business-elite position refers to the relative distribution of business elites, and the business-elite configuration in autocracies determines what kind of policy is set in the state.

3.4. General Assumptions

3.4.1. Foreign Policy and Domestic Politics

The recent scholarship on foreign policy decision-making is centered around comparative politics and makes a connection between comparative politics and international relations. In this framework, the scholars seek the motivations and determinants of foreign policy among domestic political factors. In this section, I elaborate on the first underlying assumption of the theoretical argument: foreign aid as a foreign policy tool can also be explained by domestic politics.

---

30 However, once the particular elite groups have established, this group and their practices persist until the crisis or profound changes occur in the country. Following these changes, a new elite group is created, and their practices pervade every aspect of the political life (Highley and Burton, 2006).

First, there is a consensus in the literature regarding the argument that foreign aid is a foreign policy tool due to the international nature of foreign aid. Once the state channels its economic resources to another nation as foreign aid, this transfer has consequences on multiple levels, such as interstate relations, the relationship between states and international organizations, as well as among international organizations. Relying on these levels of consequence, it is persuasive to assume that foreign aid contributes to the interaction between international actors. As a result, the governments further their aid policies by taking these foreign policy consequences into account.

Second, foreign policy and its tools are the outcomes of the various conflict of interest and institutional settings that originate from domestic politics. Once multiple within-state actors intervene in the process of policy-making, the motivations of these policies cannot be isolated from the interests of the domestic actors. Based on these two points, I assume that while foreign aid is a foreign policy tool, it is still determined by domestic politics.

3.4.2. Regime Type and Leader's Survival

If foreign policy and its tools are the outcomes of domestic politics, then the question is what types of domestic political factors contribute to these outcomes. As is detailed in the literature review section, the scholarly analyses on the domestic determinants of foreign policy and its tools are becoming broader. Still, scholars mainly focus on regime type and ideology as the most influential factors in foreign policy decision-making.

Related to the primary focus of literature, in this section, I explain the assumptions on the impact of regime type on leader's survival in their political positions. It is essential to explain how regime-type influences the leader's survival in the political office because different regime types pave different ways for the leaders to stay in office and consolidate their rule. Based on these variations, leaders develop various strategies to maintain their rule in political offices.[31]

This assumption is based on premises of international relations, particularly on the theory of Bueno De Mesquita's Selectorate Theory (De Mesquita et al., 2004). The theory offers a very insightful assumption: once in office, leaders want to remain in office (De Mesquita et al., 2004). They have a variety of tools to enhance their longevity in the office. Relying on this assumption, the theory further hypothesizes that the leader's distribution of resources helps them to stay

---

31   Some of them use elections while others pursue other strategies.

in office. These distributive resources are defined as public and private goods. The essential point of the argument is that the values of these two goods are determined by the political institutions of the state; in other words, the regime type of the state determines whether the leader needs to provide public or private goods to remain in his office.

According to Selectorate Theory, leaders in large winning coalitions (a.k.a. democracies) produce foreign policies that can yield policy concessions from other states. The leaders transform these policy concessions into public goods within their own country. Following this transformation, their supporters, who are public in democracies, can benefit from these public goods. As a result, leaders can influence the hearts and minds of the public and increase their votes in elections (De Mesquita & Smith, 2007).

In a large winning coalition, to be re-elected, leaders need larger groups of supporters than they do in small winning coalitions due to the elections. Therefore, leaders need to generate foreign policy tools to obtain policy concessions that can be transformed into public goods for the benefit of these large supporters.

Yet, this assumption also applies to autocratic countries. Not only in democracies but also in autocracies, leaders seek to stay in political office; therefore, leaders develop strategies and tools for this purpose. In democracies where the elections are not rigged, leaders who aim to be re-elected need to provide public goods. Following this premise, the leader ensures that each electorate takes advantage of the opportunities that foreign aid policies have provided. On the other hand, in non-democracies, where there is no election or free-fair election, the leader's survival depends on his/her political support coalition. That supporting coalition is mainly formed of elites. The leader needs the backing and loyalty of these elites, whereas the elites promote the continuation of the leader in office as long as they benefit from the leader.

More specifically, in non-democratic or illiberal countries where the elections are rigged, the leader's survival depends on his/her supporting coalition, which can be formed by various societal actors. However, these countries do not have a fixed level of institutionalization among themselves per se. For example, there are one-party autocracies, such as China, where leaders seek support from their political party, while there are autocracies, such as Saudi Arabia, where the leader is to be supported essentially by the royal family.

Given that there is a variation in the level of institutionalism among the authoritarian regimes, the competition between the business-elite groups might change based on this variation. To be more concrete, institutionalized autocracies have relatively larger supporting coalitions than personalistic regimes (Frantz,

2018). That might lead to a higher level of competition between the elites over resources. In turn, the level of competition between the elites influences the ways in which leaders in autocratic and illiberal regimes channel and distribute the economic resources to keep their supporters loyal. Therefore, I assume the leaders' economic policies in these countries are motivated by their aim of survival in their office.

3.4.3. Foreign Aid as a Multi-Purposed Economic Tool

Economic resources have always been at the center of the conflict of interests between and within-state actors. Therefore, the policies that regulate these economic resources are also at the center of domestic politics. In the literature, there is a consensus that economic resources and in turn, economic policies enable autocrats to stay in office and reinforce their authority. The economic tools become an instrument for the autocrats to strengthen their authority and consolidate their power in the system.

As discussed in the previous section, the leader's survival in the office depends on how much support s/he can receive from the members of the winning coalition. When economic tools are in the hands of autocratic leaders and their supporters, the leader can influence the legitimacy of his rule and prevent the opposition, whether it is another political party, movement, or coup, from rising against him. Therefore, in order to keep his legitimacy and prevent the opposition from strengthening, the leader uses economic tools and resources in a way that can enable her/him to maximize the probability of remaining in office. To do so, s/he can arrange the distribution of these economic resources on behalf of the political actors he relies on for political support.

On the other hand, if these economic resources are not used strategically by the leaders to retain and balance the elites' support, one of these two consequences might occur: First, the elites become disappointed with the leader; and as a result, they support the opposition against the leader. Second, if the elites become too powerful, their bargaining power increases, which in turn, having their support becomes too costly for the leader.[32] As a result, elites might capture political power from the hands of the leader.

Then, what is the function of foreign assistance in this bargaining process? In that context, foreign aid is an economic resource, not only for recipient countries but also for the actors within donor countries and has distributional

---

32 Acemoglu, Egorov, and Sonin (2008) explains when and how the subgroup of the supporting coalition in non-democracies can rise against the leader.

consequences for the donor's domestic actors. The donor government can decide whether to channel this economic resource as foreign aid. In autocratic institutional settings, to make a decision on channeling this economic resource as foreign aid, the leader takes into account other domestic actors. When there is an opposition, even a weak one, the leader wants to keep his/her supporters tighter and closer and distribute the economic resources toward the elites rather than the public. Losing the support of the domestic actors in his coalition might lead these actors to support the opposition. Therefore, the leader provides these supporters with benefits. Otherwise, these supporters may challenge the leaders' authority by taking the side of the opposition or basically pulling their support back.

Once foreign aid, as an economic resource, is channeled to another country, it opens a path for rent for the business elites: business elites can benefit from the aid contracts as a result of these policies and/or business elites can benefit from the increased trade relations between the countries as a result of foreign aid provision. Consequently, I assume foreign aid policy is an economic, multi-purposed tool that it is not only given for national or international purposes but within national purposes, as well.

3.5. Political Influence of Business Elites on Foreign Aid

Building on the aforementioned assumptions, what would we expect from the countries with autocratic and illiberal regimes regarding their aid policies? The main regime-related characteristic of these countries is having an autocratic or illiberal system that distinguishes them from democracies by not having strong and functional formal institutions such as competitive elections. As Frantz (2018) suggests, autocracies also differ from democracies in the clarity of decision-making procedures. In autocratic regimes, politics proceed with informal bargaining.

Although these informal bargaining processes and lack of clarity in the decision-making procedures of autocratic countries constitute some challenges for scholars of political science, we can still observe the variations within authoritarian regimes. As Geddes (1999) and Gandhi (2008) demonstrate, authoritarian countries differ in their institutional settings. One cannot categorize and examine Mexico under the Institutional Revolutionary Party (PRI) and Saudi Arabia under King Salman bin Abdul Aziz El Saud, with the royal family at the same level. Their level of institutionalization, the political orientation of the elites, the size of the supporting coalition, the decision-making procedure, number and influence of the actors in decision-making are all different.

It is not only the autocratic countries that have an informal bargaining process, however. Illiberal regimes, the countries that have elections, can also rely on the informal bargaining process when they do not carry the liberal characteristics of democracy, such as the protection of economic, civil, and religious liberties. The absence of these liberties and competitiveness or fairness in the elections (even when there are elections) indicates that the leader relies on the support of elites more than the public as his/her supporters.[33] Russia, under the rule of Putin, is one of the common examples of these regime types.[34]

In this respect, autocracy can be defined as the regime type where there are no fairly competitive elections on the one hand but can be categorized differently depending on the level of institutionalization on the other. Illiberal democracy can be defined as the regime type where there are elections but lack or are short of civil liberties and fairness in the elections. Following that, it is highly persuasive to argue that as the level of institutionalization between the countries with these regime types varies, actors within the decision-making process vary, paving the way for different policy outcomes.

Furthermore, the level of institutionalization in these regimes determines the competition of elites in these countries. The greater level of institutionalization leads to a greater level of competition among the business elites. Therefore, instead of distinguishing between full, institutionalized autocracies and between illiberal democracies and autocracies, I will focus on the level of competition within elite configuration in this study. The competition in the ladder of institutionalism should be reflected in the configuration of the elites.

3.5.1. The Influence of Business Elites on Donorship

Up to this section, the assumptions that base the theoretical argument on autocratic and illiberal countries' aid policies have been explained. As discussed in the previous section, foreign aid policies can be at the center of conflict of interest between the domestic actors, that can be used by the leader to strengthen

---

33   The elections can even be a tool for elite management. Blaydes (2008) argues, for example, in Egypt the parliamentary elections are used as a tool for the distributions of rents and promotions to the politically influential business groups.

34   There are different approaches regarding these regimes, though. Some scholars call them as "competitive authoritarian" regimes (Levitsky & Way, 2002) whereas some of them call "hybrid regimes" and the others call semiauthoritarianism (Ottoway, 2003). I will follow the concept of illiberal democracies (Zakaria, 1997) mainly for the operationalization purposes.

his power. With regard to that, it is essential to discuss which domestic actors influence the motivations and preferences of the leader on aid giving.

A critical characteristic of autocratic and illiberal regimes is that the leaders in these regimes are not elected by elections or at least by competitive and fair elections, so they are not highly accountable to and dependent on the electorate. When there are no competitive elections, politicians are unlikely to have a tendency to provide public goods. In other words, in those regimes, leaders might not prefer channel the economic resources to the public to enhance the social welfare of citizens unless their survivals in their rules depend on the public's choices.

Another critical characteristic of an autocratic and illiberal rule is that the policy decisions are made within a supporting coalition relative to democracies. With respect to this, while the decisions are made with majority rule in democracies, in autocracies, and illiberal regimes, the leader and his/her supporting coalition are responsible for policy-making. The size of this coalition varies depending on the level of institutionalization of the regime.

Given that the leaders are not accountable to their electorates in these regimes, and the policy-making decisions are concerned by their small coalition size, it can be inferred that foreign aid policies also lay in the interplay of the leader and the members of supporting coalitions.

Then, the question is who the members of the supporting coalition of the leader in autocracies and illiberal regimes are. There is an agreement in the literature that the supporting coalitions of autocratic leaders are formed of political, military, and economic elites. More specifically, these elites can be high-ranking military officers, civil political officers, business elites, and relatives of the leader. However, once the economic policies are involved in the process, I argue that business elites that are in the supporting coalition are more likely to be active in the policy-making process and are more influential on the outcome on behalf of the aid giving.

Yet, one question remains: why and how do these business elites influence foreign aid policy-making? One possible answer lays at the interaction between the business elites and the leader in charge of aid policies. In autocratic countries, leaders and these business elites have two-way- relationships. In one way, these business elites can support the leader by financing his campaign, offering the necessary technology and innovation that can help the leader to win the election or consolidate his power without the election, and persuading the other elites to be supportive of the leader. However, to maximize their benefits, these business elites usually seek something in return. Looking at this relationship from the other way around, the leader can provide these elites with some economic or institutional benefits in return for their support.

In this context, foreign aid is an economic policy that business elites can benefit from if the leader is willing to provide it for the business elites. Yet, not all business elites would be equally influential in foreign aid policy-making. Some business groups might gain relatively more benefits in foreign aid policies compared to others. To understand which group can be influential, it is important to know what exactly business elites can gain from aid policies in exchange for their support.

First, as a result of foreign aid, interstate trade, and foreign direct investment opportunities arise, and certain companies, specifically if they are export and import-oriented, can gain access to the international market.[35] For example, the interest of the Chinese government in Africa and Chinese aid provision has been seen as a way to increase trade links. Second, with foreign aid, the leaders provide an opportunity for the companies to be the contractor of foreign aid projects. To implement these projects, certain companies receive contracts and are even funded by the state. For example, again in China, many aid projects are implemented by state-owned companies (SOEs) (Dreher et al., 2017; Breslin, 2013).

In either scenario, it is plausible that foreign aid is provided to help the *trade-oriented domestic business elite* in exchange for their support to the leader. It can happen in two ways. First, business elites can persuade the leader to develop foreign aid policies. Second, the leader might decide to provide foreign aid but wants to reward the business elites with opportunities that foreign aid provides. In either case, the trade-oriented business elites should have an influence on politics because otherwise, the leader does not need to provide them with any benefits. Therefore, I hypothesize the followings:

Hypothesis 1a: Autocratic and illiberal regimes with a high degree of political influence from the export-oriented business elite are more likely to provide foreign aid than other autocratic and illiberal regimes.

---

35   The relationship between aid and trade has been discussed in many studies. Accordingly, aid flows can affect trade flows in three ways. Aid flows can increase the trade because aid can increase the economic development in the recipient country; as a result, the recipient country might create a market for the trade. Second, aid can be directly tied to the trade. Third, as a result of aid provision, the bilateral economic and political relationships between the donor and recipient can be reinforced. Foreign aid can do either one of them or combination of them (Suwa-Eisenmann & Verdier, 2007).

Hypothesis 1a: Autocratic and illiberal regimes with a high degree of political influence from the export-oriented business elites are more likely to provide a higher amount of foreign aid than other autocratic and illiberal regimes.

3.5.2. Configuration of Business Elites on Foreign Aid Preferences

Once an autocratic country becomes a donor as a result of the influence of export-oriented business elites, the second step is the determination of preferences over these aid policies. That being said, not every foreign aid preference aligns with a particular business interest. However, in autocracies, where there is intra-elite competition between the actors, leaders are more sensitive to the demands of business elites since they need to keep these elites on their sides. Otherwise, these elites might support the opposition.

In this structure, the configuration and market structure of the business elites that compete for the aid projects contracts and the potential trade cooperation with the recipient become significant in the selection of the recipient country, how many projects and how much value of aid is provided, what type of aid and in which sector it is provided. For example, if the market structure has an oligopolistic or monopolistic characteristic where one or a few business elites dominate the economy, these dominant business elites might leave little room for the smaller business firms to win aid project contracts. Moreover, this dominant business group is more likely to be within the supporting coalition of the leader. Hence, when there is a dominant business group, the leader might decide to provide higher-value of projects so that the dominant business group can be awarded with the contracts of these higher amount projects. For one example, as a result of the economic elite transformation in Turkey under the rule of AKP, the construction and energy industries have become the driving force of the nation's economy. This transformation is also reflected in Turkish foreign assistance. The reports of the Turkish official Aid Agency (TIKA) demonstrate that Turkey is involved in many aid projects in the construction sector, such as the construction and renovation of bridges, mosques, schools, and hospitals.[36]

On the contrary, if there is more differentiation among business elites with regard to their dominance in the economy, the policy-making process might be complicated as the competition between the business elites rises. This is also reflected in the value of aid projects since the leader has to provide sufficient

---

36   See TIKA's reports for more detailed information from its website: http://www.tika. gov.tr/tr/yayin/liste/turkiye_kalkinma_yardimlari_raporlari-24.

benefits for the competitive business elites and share these opportunities among different business-elite groups. Therefore, I hypothesize:

Hypothesis 2a: The lower the equality in business-elite configuration, the higher the number of projects with a high value of each will be provided from the donors with autocratic and illiberal regime types.

Hypothesis 2b: The higher the equality in business-elite configuration, the higher the number of aid projects with a low value of each will be provided from the donors with autocratic and illiberal regime types.

In addition to the number and value of the projects in given aid, the configuration of business elites might also influence the type of sector in which the aid is given. If foreign aid is given to provide benefits for the trade-oriented domestic business elites in exchange for their support to the leader, then the type of sector needs to be aligned with the configuration of business-elite groups. To be more concrete, if there is a dominant business group in the market economy, then the sectors in which aid is given might not demonstrate variation since aid is given on the sector of this dominant business elite. On the other hand, if there is more competition between the elites, in other words, if there is more differentiation within the configuration of the business groups, the distribution of the aid projects is shaped as an alignment of this distribution.

Hypothesis 3: The greater the equality in the business-elite configuration, the more variation in the sectors of foreign aid.

In addition to the provision of the number and type of the projects, when there is less competition over the opportunities among the business elites as a result of foreign aid projects, the leader also creates some opportunity for these business elites by providing foreign aid to the countries where the dominant business group's interest lies. If one business group is dominant in the economy, the leader might target specific countries that can increase the trade opportunity for this group. Therefore, recipient countries are higher-income or resource-rich countries. Targeting resource-rich countries as aid recipients might bring some export-import opportunities for the business elites. On the contrary, when there is a differentiation among the business-elite groups, the leader might be indifferent about the aid recipients due to the competition between the elites. To test this argument, I also hypothesize:

Hypothesis 4a: Autocratic and illiberal donors with a more dominant business-elite structure are more likely to target resource-rich and middle-income countries as their aid recipients.

Hypothesis 4b: Autocratic and illiberal donors with greater equality in the business-elite configuration are more likely to target low-income countries as their aid recipients.

In light of these explanations and hypothesis, I expect that the autocracies and illiberal countries where the political influence of business elites is higher, become donors. However, their preferences over aid policies are determined by the configuration of business elites. Autocracies with a more equal business-elite structure tend to provide a higher number of projects, each with a lower amount, to the countries in need. Autocracies with highly dominant business-elite structures tend to provide a smaller number of projects, each with a higher amount, to resource-rich countries.

The following chapters of the book will test these hypotheses empirically by using quantitative methodology and discuss the results.

Chapter 4 Donor Motivations in Illiberal and Autocratic Regimes

Abstract: Why do the non-democratic or illiberal regimes provide foreign aid? This chapter of the book examines the theoretical argument that politically influential business elites motivate non-democratic or illiberal donors to provide foreign aid. Further, this chapter also tests if the countries in which the business elites are more influential in politics are more likely to provide aid. To test the hypothesis, the chapter benefits from the data of the OECD, AidData, and Enterprise Survey. The results of the analysis indicate that non-democratic or illiberal regimes are more likely to be donors and more likely to provide higher amounts of foreign aid in the case they have more politically influential firms.

Keywords: Politically Influential Business Elite, Politically Connected Firms, Donorship, Enterprise Survey

4.1. Introduction

In the previous chapter, I explained the theoretical approach regarding the motivation and preferences of autocratic and illiberal governments for aid giving. As discussed in the theory chapter, autocratic and illiberal governments are driven for aid giving due to the nature of the relationship between the government and politically influential business elites. Therefore, as stated in hypothesis 1a in the third chapter, it can be expected that autocratic and illiberal regimes with greater political influence from the export-oriented business elites are more likely to be donors. Furthermore, as stated in hypothesis 1b, autocratic and illiberal regimes with greater political influence from the export-oriented business elites are more likely to provide a higher amount of assistance than autocratic and illiberal regimes with lower political influence from the export-oriented business elites.

This chapter focuses on the relationship between the political influence of the business elites and the foreign aid motivation of non-democratic countries and discusses the data, methodology, and tests used to examine this relationship. First, I will explain the dependent, independent, and control variables, along with describing the data used for the variables. In addition, I will present and discuss the data sources gathered for the empirical analysis in this chapter.

Second, I will outline the estimation strategies to test the relationship between the political influence of export-oriented business elites and the aid motivation of non-democratic countries. Lastly, I will present and discuss the results of these estimations and robustness tests.

4.2. Data

To test the relationship between the political influence of export-oriented business elites and foreign assistance initiation of the autocratic and illiberal governments, the dependent variables are defined as *donorship, amount of foreign assistance,* and *generosity of the donor.* The independent variables are the measures of the political influence of the export-oriented business elites: corruption perception of the export-oriented firms and corruption perception of the export-oriented firms relative to the real level of corruption in the country. A detailed breakdown of the variables used in this analysis can be seen in Table 4.1 at the end of the "data" section.

4.2.1. Dependent Variables

Because the focus of this book, and hypothesis 1, is aid giving, dependent variables are defined as the measures of "aid giving." Three dependent variables are considered in this analysis to measure "aid giving." The first one is the *donorship* variable, which measures whether the illiberal or autocratic country provides aid or not in a given year. It is the most direct measure of aid giving. The second dependent variable, the *amount of aid*, measures the amount of assistance a country provides in a given year. The reason for taking this variable into account is that the political influence of business elites is not only influential solely on the provision of aid, but they might also influence how much aid is given. To be more specific, the amount of assistance is part of aid giving because there is a substantive difference between giving one dollar foreign assistance and one million dollar assistance. More amount of aid requires higher motivation. In addition to donorship and aid amount variables, this study uses the *generosity* variable, which measures the amount of aid relative to the gross national income (GNI) of the country, as the third dependent variable. This dependent variable enables the study to examine not only how much these countries provide aid but also how much they provide aid relative to their GNI. While the amount of aid matters for the donors, its importance varies depending on the size of their economy. A higher amount of aid requires higher motivation from smaller economies than it does from larger ones.

Throughout this empirical chapter, I use two different databases to measure the dependent variables: OECD's QWIDS Query Wizard for International

Development Statistics (OECD Development Assistance Database) (OECD, 2019d) and AidData, A Research Lab at William's Mary, Core Research Release, Version 3.1 database (AidData, 2017a). These databases are the most extensive and reliable sources that provide information about the assistance of autocratic and illiberal countries. The first database, which is from OECD, is maintained by OECD's International Development Statistics and prepared based on the country's reports to the OECD on official development assistance. The second one, AidData, is maintained by Harvard University's William & Mary Research Center. William & Mary Research Center collects the aid data for the AidData database from the OECD's data on official development assistance, the country's own official reports, and newspapers on foreign assistance.

My first dependent variable, *donorship*, is coded based on these two databases: OECD and AidData. OECD International Development Statistics suggests information for official development assistance (ODA) and OOF flows. OECD defines ODA as "government aid designed to promote the economic development and welfare of developing countries" (OECD, 2019b). This definition excludes loans and credits for military purposes from the ODA category. Loans with grant elements of at least 25 percent of the total are still considered ODA, whereas loans with grant elements less than 25 percent of the total are excluded from the ODA. ODA can be provided bilaterally but can still be channeled through a multilateral development agency such as the United Nations or the World Bank. All technical assistance is included in the aid definition of OECD. This database gives information about aid-related activities of all DAC and some non-DAC donors between the years of 1960 and 2017.

The AidData's Core Research Release, Version 3.1 thin version; on the other hand, suggests project-level data by using the definition of OECD's Official Development Assistance. This database includes aid commitment information for over 1.5 million development finance activities funded between 1947 and 2013, covers 96 donors, and includes ODA, OOF flows, Equity Investments, and Export Credits (AidData, 2017a).

Relying on the information in these two databases, donorship has been coded as a binary variable and determined based on whether or not these databases have information about the country's aid in a given year. If either of the databases has information about the aid, then the value of the variable is aid given. If neither of these databases has information about the foreign aid by country in a given year, then the variable is coded as aid is not given.

The second dependent variable in the analysis is the *amount of aid* a non-democratic country provides in a given year. Only OECD's Official Development Assistance database is used for this variable in order to ensure consistency on the aid amount. OECD's database presents the aid amount information for each country-year, both as a commitment and a disbursement amount (OECD, 2019a). I use the disbursement amount, which is calculated in million dollars. Then, I take the log of the aid amount for the empirical test for each country-year. In consequence, unlike the first dependent variable, the second dependent variable is the continuous level of measurement, given that it is the log version of the dollar amount of foreign aid.

The third dependent variable measures the *generosity* of the countries. It is calculated based on the amount of foreign aid as a percentage of the GNI of the donor country. In order to construct this variable, I have collected the GNI level of countries from the OECD database (OECD, 2019c) for each year and computed the generosity variable as the amount of aid/GNI. As a result, I have obtained continuous measurements for this variable, which might change between 0 and 100 depending on the GNI share of donors' assistance.

4.2.2. Independent Variables

I use one type of independent variable with three different measures. According to the hypothesis, a high-political influence of export-oriented business elites would drive governments with autocratic and illiberal regime types to provide foreign assistance and a high amount of foreign assistance. Therefore, the primary explanatory variable is identified as the *political influence of export-oriented business elites.* In terms of measuring the political influence of export-oriented business elites, I use three different measures: Perception of Corruption of Firms,[37] Perception of Corruption of Firms Relative to the Political Corruption Level,[38] and Perception of Corruption of Firms Relative to the Public Sector Corruption Level[39] in a country-year.

Measurement of Political Influence of Business Elites and Enterprise Survey

Because there is no direct measure of the political influence of export-oriented business elites, it is imperative to use the most valid measure for this variable, even if it is an indirect measure. The lack of sufficient databases of the autocratic countries, particularly of their businesses and firm-level surveys, makes

---

37   Used as *Corruption Perception of Firms* in the tests.
38   Used as *Real Corruption Perception of Firms* in the tests.
39   Used as *Real Corruption Perception of Firms2* in the tests.

measuring the political influence of business elites more challenging. However, the Enterprise Survey offers a detailed firm-level survey for most of the autocratic countries.

Hence, my explanatory variable, which measures the political influence of the export-oriented business elites, is from the Enterprise Survey of the World Bank. Enterprise Survey is based on the surveys of 135,000 firms in 139 countries, which are primarily non-democracies, between 2002 and 2016. It includes different information about the firms in non-democratic countries regarding their sizes, major challenges, and their biggest obstacles in their businesses (Enterprise Survey, 2019).

In the Enterprise Survey, the measure I use for the political influence of export-oriented business elites is the *export-oriented firms' perception of corruption* in the country-year period. The perception of corruption variable is the percentage of export-oriented firms that identify corruption as the major constraint for their businesses in each country. If the firms have political influence in the country, then they would not recognize the corruption in their government. Therefore, I would expect a negative correlation between this explanatory variable and the dependent variable. To be more precise, lower values in the perception of corruption of the firms translate to the higher political influence of firms.

On the other hand, this variable does not directly measure the firms' perception of corruption relative to the real level of corruption in the country. To be more precise, firms, in other words, business elites in this context, might not be perceiving any corruption and believe that corruption is not a major constraint for their businesses. However, this belief might not occur because they have political relations or political influence on government but because there, indeed, is not a high level of corruption in the country. Then, the perception of corruption would be just the reflection of the existing situation, not the reflection of firms' political influence. In order to solve this issue, I also create two additional explanatory variables that measure the perception of corruption, depending on the real level of corruption in the country.

These variables are created from the residuals of firms' perception of corruption variable relative to the countries' corruption level variable by regressing the perception of corruption on the real level of corruption in the country. To create these variables, I use the political corruption and public sector corruption indexes from the V-Dem (Coppedge et al., 2018a, 2018b; Pemstein et al., 2019) and re-test the models. The regression results and figures of residuals can be found in the section for estimation strategies and tests.

While Enterprise Survey offers the most extensive database for business in non-democratic countries, this dataset has two main drawbacks. One drawback of Enterprise Survey is that the survey data is available only once or twice per country in the period between 2002 and 2016, which reduces the sample size because there are only one or two observations for each country between these years. Another drawback is that it does not include survey information for a few of the donor Arab countries, such as Saudi Arabia and the United Arab Emirates. The lack of data for these countries causes a loss of information in the analysis of these countries. Moreover, this absence of information on these countries becomes an even more serious issue considering that these countries are non-democratic and also sizable donors. Once these countries are included in the Enterprise Survey database in the future, the measures from this dataset will be more reliable for this study's purposes.

4.2.3. Control Variables

A range of control variables is included in the analysis. These variables are the log of GDP per capita, log of population, log of economic growth as a percentage of GDP, and total natural resources as a percentage of GDP from the World Bank's database (World Bank, 2018a, 2018b, 2018c, 2018d); OECD membership from the OECD's website (OECD, 2019e), WTO/GATT membership from the WTO's website (WTO, 2019); and level of neopatrimonialism in a country and polity score of a country from Variety of Democracies (V-Dem) database (Coppedge et al., 2018a; Pemstein et al., 2019).

These variables are crucial to be included in the analysis, given that their effects on the provision of foreign aid are not very clear. The population of countries might be negatively influencing the provision of foreign aid, given that governments might keep their resources for their nations rather than channeling these economic resources to another nation. On the other hand, a high population might increase the likelihood of aid provision when a high population necessitates more policy concessions from other countries as a result of foreign aid provision. GDP's impact on foreign aid provision is more obvious; however, neither all the countries with high GDPs provide aid nor the countries with middle income, such as Turkey, Brazil, and India, refrain from providing foreign aid. In terms of natural resources, it can be expected that countries with high natural resources might help others with these resources; however, the governments might also prefer keeping these natural resources for their own nation or for private benefits in non-democracies.

The other control variables, membership of OECD and membership of WTO/GATT, also have an ambiguous relationship with the provision of foreign aid, although it is understandable that membership to those organizations is a sign for willingness to international cooperation. Nonetheless, it does not provide sufficient evidence for aid provision. Until recently, only the OECD's DAC members were providing foreign assistance. Yet, we have begun to see non-DAC members and even non-OECD members such as Saudi Arabia and the United Arab Emirates as donors and also among the most prominent donors. Similarly, Saudi Arabia has been a member of the WTO since 2005, even though it has been assisting long before its membership to the WTO since the 1970s. Both WTO membership and OECD membership variables are binary and coded as 0 for not being a member and 1 for being a member in a given year.

I have also included a couple of institutional variables from the V-Dem database, such as the level of neopatrimonialism and polity score variables. The level of neopatrimonialism variable measures the neopatrimonial rule in a country, which is defined as the reflection of "the idea that personalistic forms of authority pervade formal regime institutions" (Clapham, 1985; Coppedge et al., 2018b). According to this measurement, the rule is neopatrimonial if there are "clientelistic political relationships, strong and unconstrained presidents, and the use of public resources for political legitimation" (Bratton & Van de Walle, 1997).[40] The variable is continuous between 0 and 1, and higher values indicate higher levels of neopatrimonialism. The Polity variable is the regime score of the country in a given year and comes from the measure of the Polity IV dataset but is taken from V-Dem. It measures the regime score between –10 and 10 from full autocratic to full democratic (Coppedge et al., 2018a; Pemstein et al., 2019). Table 4.1 presents the variable names, operationalizations and sources used in the tests.

---

40 V-Dem constructs this variable based on "the Bayesian Factor Analysis of 16 indicators representing the factors of clientelistic political relationships, strong presidents and use of public resources for political legitimation and the 16 indicators are: vote buying (v2elvotbuy), particularistic vs. public goods (v2dlencmps), party linkages (v2psprlnks), executive respects constitution (v2exrescon), executive oversight (v2lgotovst), legislature controls resources (v2lgfunds), legislature investigates the executive in practice (v2lginvstp), high court independence (V2juhcind), low court independence (v2jucnind), compliance with high court (v2juhccomp), compliance with judiciary (v2jucomp), electoral management body autonomy (v2elembaut), executive embezzlement and theft (v2exembez), executive bribes and corrupt exchanges (v2exbribe), legislative corruption (v2lgcrrpt) and judicial corruption (v2jucorrdc)" (Coppedge et al., 2018b)

Table 4.1. Variable Names, Operationalizations, and Sources

Variable Names	Operationalizations	Sources
Donorship	Is aid given? If a country provides aid in a given year. 0 Aid is not provided 1 Aid is provided	OECD, (2017, 2019d), AidData (2017a)
lnAid	Natural log of amount of aid provided in a given country-year in U.S. million dollars at current prices.	OECD (2017, 2019d)
Aid As a Share (%GNI)	Amount of foreign assistance provided in a year as a share of GNI.	OECD (2019d)
Perception Corruption of Firms	Percentage of firms identifying corruption as the major constraint for their businesses in the country-year.	Enterprise Survey (2019), (Coppedge et al., 2018a; Pemstein et al., 2019)
Real Perception Corruption	Residuals of Percentage of firms identifying corruption as the major constraint for their businesses in the country- year relative to the real perception of political corruption a country-year.	Enterprise Survey (2019), (Coppedge et al., 2018a; Pemstein et al., 2019)
Real Perception Corruption2	Residuals of Percentage of firms identifying corruption as the major constraint for their businesses in the country- year relative to the real perception of public sector corruption a country- year.	Enterprise Survey (2019), (Coppedge et al., 2018a; Pemstein et al., 2019)
lnGDP	Natural log of gross domestic product per capita in U.S. million dollars at current prices.	World Bank (2018a)
lnGrowth	Natural log of GDP growth of a country in a given year.	World Bank (2018c)
OECD membership	Is the country an OECD member? If a country is an OECD member in a given year. 0 not an OECD member in a given year 1 an OECD member in a given year	OECD (2019e)
WTO membership	Is the country a WTO member? If a country is a WTO member in a given year. 0 not a WTO member in a given year 1 a WTO member in a given year	WTO (2019)
lnPopulation	Natural log of the population of a country in a given year.	World Bank (2018b)
Resources	Total natural resources as a share of the GDP of a country in a given year.	World Bank (2018d)

Table 4.1. Continued

Neopatrimnial	Country's level of Neopatrimonialism Continuous measure between 0 and 1	(Coppedge et al., 2018a; Pemstein et al., 2019)
Polity	Country's regime-type score between −10 and 10.	(Coppedge et al., 2018a; Pemstein et al., 2019)

4.3. Estimation Strategy and Tests

Analyzing the motivation of non-democratic or illiberal donors requires several steps, from preliminary data reconfiguration to post-estimation strategies. Preliminary data operations include reconfiguration and collapse of the databases and operationalization of the variables so that the analyses can be implemented with these obtained variables. Then, the analyses are implemented with the proper tests depending on the level of measurements of the dependent variables. Following the tests, robustness analysis is required to check the robustness of the findings as post-estimation strategies.

As a first step, I had to reconfigure the databases, which included selecting autocratic and illiberal countries for the analysis and creating a proper measure for dependent variables and independent variables. In order to select the autocratic and illiberal countries for the analysis, I have utilized the World Bank's country list and then filtered the autocratic and illiberal countries based on the V-Dem regime-type measure. V-Dem has a "regimes of the world (v2x_regime)" variable with four different categories: 1 = closed autocracy, 2 = electoral autocracy, 3 = electoral democracy, 4 = liberal democracy (Coppedge et al., 2018b). In this categorization, I have filtered out the liberal democracies (code 4) and missing cases and kept the other categories, including electoral democracies, in the database because electoral democracies do not have a satisfying level of liberal component in their access to justice, transparent law enforcement and the liberal principles of respect for personal liberties, the rule of law, and judicial as well as legislative constraints on the executive. Because aid is characterized by liberal ideology, I am interested in why illiberal or autocratic regimes give foreign assistance. Based on this selection, I obtained a country-year level dataset for autocratic and illiberal countries between 2002 and 2017, having 188 observations. The list of the country-years that are included in the analysis can be found in the appendix in Table A.1.

For the first dependent variable, which is donorship, I have checked both OECD's and AidData's databases to investigate if the country has provided foreign assistance in a given year. If none of these databases has information, then I have coded the donorship as 0 (aid is not given). If either of these datasets has information about the country's foreign aid in a given year, I have coded the variable as 1 (aid is given). OECD has an additional database for the countries which do not report to OECD, such as Brazil, Mexico, and China. This small database includes information about these countries' assistance that is gathered from their governmental reports. If the country has information in this database, I have still coded them as 1 (aid is given). For the second dependent variable (aid amount), I have logged the data of aid amount gathered from OECD's database. For the third dependent variable, generosity (aid as a share of GNI), I have obtained the GNI of countries from the OECD and divided the aid amount by their GNI.[41]

In terms of explanatory variables, the Enterprise Survey did not require much work since it already has a variable that measures the percentages of export-oriented firms which identify corruption as a major obstacle for their firms. Besides, this database includes data mostly from autocratic and illiberal countries. I have just matched the data from the Enterprise Survey with the filtered country-year data I gathered. However, as explained above, this variable only measures the corruption perception of the export-oriented firms in the country-year. Therefore, I had to develop new measurements by estimating the perception of corruption relative to the real corruption level in the country. In order to do that, I have run two separate OLS regression analyses by placing the corruption perception of firms variable as a dependent variable and the real level of corruption as an independent variable.

The V-Dem database has three different measures for the level of corruption in a country. One of them is the Transparency International Index. However, this variable measures the public perception, therefore, is not of interest. The second variable for the level of corruption is the political corruption variable. It does not measure the perception, but the corruption in the political sphere, so I use this variable for the first regression analysis. Also, V-Dem's third corruption variable is the level of corruption in the public sector. I also use this variable in the second regression analysis to obtain the real corruption perception of firms variable estimated based on the real level of corruption in the country in a given year. After running the regression tests, I have predicted the residuals and created new

---

41   Generosity=Aid Amount/Gross National Income.

Table 4.2. OLS Analysis of Perception of Corruption

	Corruption Perception of Firms	Corruption Perception of Firms
Political Corruption	34.48***	
	(4.31)	
Public Sector Corruption		29.16***
		(3.88)
Constant	14.61**	19.47***
	(2.61)	(3.91)
Observations	188	188
Adjusted R^2	0.086	0.070

t statistics in parentheses
*$p < 0.05$, **$p < 0.01$, ***$p < 0.001$

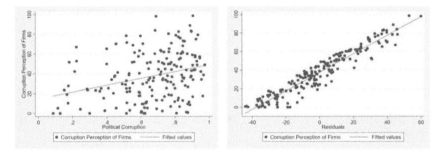

Figure 4.1. Relationship and Residuals of Corruption Perception of Firms and Real Level of Political Corruption

variables from these variables. Table 4.2 presents the regression results, while Figures 4.1 and 4.2 present the residuals and fitted value lines for both "real" corruption perception of the export-oriented firms variables.

After obtaining the measure for the political influence of export-oriented business elites from the real level of corruption variables and matching these variables in the dataset, I reconfigure the dataset by organizing control variables from the other databases, such as World Bank, as explained above. Summary statistics for all variables can be seen in Table 4.3.

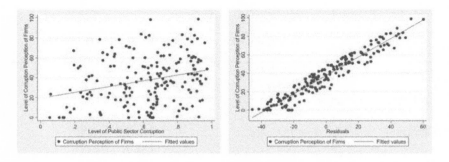

Figure 4.2. Relationship and Residuals of Corruption Perception of Firms and Real Level of Public Sector Corruption

Table 4.3. Descriptive Statistics

variable	count	mean	sd	min	max
Donorship	2,305	.0950108	.29322935	0	1
lnAid	2,305	.4638228	1.614529	0	9.002322
Aid as a Share	2,196	.0001753	.0009938	0	.0136688
Corruption Perception of Firms	188	37.63936	24.02772	0	98.8
Real Corruption Perception of Firms	188	−0.0000000529	22.91071	−44.10375	59.93162
Real Corruption Perception of Firms2	188	−0.0000000225	23.11051	−45.70204	60.13411
lnGDP	2,248	7.673699	1.314473	4.712799	11.39149
lnGrowth	2,005	1.478718	.8005514	11.30382	21.04997
lnPopulation	2,229	16.06222	1.672987	11.30382	21.04997
Resources	2,242	11.26709	13.79553	0	86.45256
WTO membership	2,305	.7245119	.4468568	0	1
OECD membership	2,305	.0229935	.1499151	0	1
Neopatrimonial	2,305	.4125853	.2421474	0	1
Polity	1,902	1.881178	6.235478	−10	10

4.4. Results

To test the relationship between independent and dependent variables, I employ a series of analyses depending on the level of measurement of the dependent variables. First, I employ logit analysis with the donorship variable. Then I continue with OLS analysis with the aid amount variable. Following these

Table 4.4. Logit Analysis of Whether Aid Is Given

	Model 1	Model 2	Model 3
Donorship			
Corruption Perception of Firms	−0.0548*	−0.0553*	−0.0576*
	(−2.05)	(−2.05)	(−2.02)
lnGDP	2.532**	2.411**	2.965**
	(3.26)	(2.75)	(2.85)
lnPopulation	1.112**	1.078**	1.287**
	(3.04)	(2.83)	(2.96)
WTO membership	−2.366	−2.313	−2.252
	(−1.38)	(−1.34)	(−1.10)
Resources	0.0332	0.0345	0.0629
	(0.82)	(0.84)	(1.11)
lnGrowth	−0.608	−0.578	−0.733
	(−1.24)	(−1.15)	(−1.31)
Polity	0.199	0.188	−0.0784
	(1.65)	(1.49)	(−0.39)
OECD membership		0.378	−0.626
		(0.27)	(−0.42)
Neopatrimonial			8.486
			(1.79)
Constant	−39.48***	−37.93**	−49.46**
	(−3.76)	(−3.27)	(−3.23)
Observations	148	148	148
Pseudo R^2	0.526	0.527	0.580

t statistics in parentheses
*$p < 0.05$, **$p < 0.01$, ***$p < 0.001$

two analyses, I employ the Heckman Selection test for both of the dependent variables aiming to reduce any potential bias in the logit and OLS estimates. After the Heckman Selection analyses, I employ the same series of analyses with the real corruption perception of export-oriented firms variables. This includes both real corruption perception of firms and real corruption perception of firms2 variables.

The first model is the logit regression on aid giving. The second and third models include additional control variables in the logit analysis in order to see if there will be any changes with the additional control variables. The results of these models can be seen in Table 4.4.

Table 4.4 demonstrates the results based on the question of whether countries provide any aid or not. Model 1 uses the firms' perception of corruption as an explanatory variable. The theoretical argument suggests that countries with illiberal and autocratic regimes are most likely to give foreign aid (Donorship) when export-oriented firms' perception of corruption is low. In other words, considering that firms' perception of corruption measures the political influence of export-oriented business elites in a negative way, countries with illiberal and autocratic regimes are most likely to give foreign aid when export-oriented firms' political influence increases. The significant negative coefficient on the perception of corruption supports this argument, even after including additional control variables.

In addition to the corruption perception variable, in all three models, GDP and population variables are significant, referring to the fact that higher GDP and higher population increase the probability of aid giving.

Besides the aid giving, in the following models, I analyze the political influence of export-oriented analysis on the given aid amount. The fourth model is the OLS regression of the aid amount. The fifth and sixth models include additional control variables to see if any changes with additional control variables will occur. The results can be seen in Table 4.5.

Table 4.5 presents the results based on the question of whether countries' amount of aid change depending on the political influence of export-oriented business elites. Again, my theory suggests that as the political influence of export-oriented business elites' increases, the countries with illiberal and autocratic regimes, are more likely to provide larger amounts of foreign aid. The results in Table 4.5 supports this hypothesis. In Model 4, the perception of corruption by firms is significant with a negative coefficient estimate, indicating that as the perception of corruption decreases, in other words, the political influence of the export-oriented business increases, the amount of aid provision increases. In addition to the primary explanatory variable, GDP and population variables are significant on aid amount, similarly to the variable of aid giving. However, unlike the aid-giving models, OECD membership is also significant on aid amount.

While OLS regression analysis supports the hypothesis, some scholars argue that OLS can give biased results if the dependent variables are restricted with some values. In the analysis of this study, the dependent variable is bounded with 0 value since the aid amount cannot be lower than 0 amount. In order to see if the results of the OLS estimates are biased and to suggest a more complementary approach, I employ Heckman Selection analysis. Heckman's model has two stages and consists of both a binary dependent variable stage and a continuous dependent variable stage. Heckman analysis is employed with and without

Table 4.5. OLS Analysis of Amount of Given Aid

	Model 4	Model 5	Model 6
Corruption Perception of Firms	−0.0110*	−0.0101*	−0.00965*
	(−2.30)	(−2.25)	(−2.10)
lnGDP	0.540***	0.389***	0.382***
	(4.79)	(3.50)	(3.40)
lnPopulation	0.420***	0.350***	0.354***
	(5.23)	(4.55)	(4.56)
WTO membership	0.0924	0.0849	0.0740
	(0.28)	(0.28)	(0.24)
Resources	0.000340	0.00152	0.00243
	(0.03)	(0.14)	(0.22)
lnGrowth	−0.276	−0.181	−0.194
	(−1.65)	(−1.13)	(−1.20)
Polity	0.00507	−0.00712	−0.0148
	(0.21)	(−0.31)	(−0.55)
OECD membership		2.561***	2.518***
		(4.42)	(4.29)
Neopatrimonial			0.320
			(0.52)
Constant	−9.863***	−7.819***	−7.928***
	(−6.12)	(−4.94)	(−4.95)
Observations	148	148	148
Adjusted R^2	0.262	0.349	0.345

t statistics in parentheses
*$p < 0.05$, **$p < 0.01$, ***$p < 0.001$

additional control variables in the seventh and eight models. The results can be seen in Table 4.6.

Table 4.6 presents the results based on whether countries provide any aid and how much aid is provided. Both Models 7 and 8 of Heckman analysis verify the results of logit and OLS regressions. Both models support the theoretical argument suggesting that countries with illiberal and autocratic regimes are most likely to give foreign aid (Donorship) and provide higher assistance when export-oriented firms' perception of corruption is low. In sum, we can conclude that the results of logit and OLS are not biased. On the other hand, the Mills ratio of the Heckman Selection model is not significant. This also shows that OLS results would not be biased. However, it might also be because of the low number of observations on the selection stage of the Heckman model.

Table 4.6. Heckman Analysis of Donorship and Amount of Given Aid

	Model 7: Amount of Given Aid	Model 8: Amount of Given Aid	Model 7: Is Aid Given	Model 8: Is Aid Given
Corruption Perception of Firms	-0.0392*	-0.0323**	-0.0343*	-0.0351*
	(-2.03)	(-2.60)	(-2.23)	(-2.13)
lnGDP	1.127	0.788*	1.388**	1.570**
	(1.07)	(1.98)	(3.24)	(2.85)
lnPopulation	1.251***	1.163***	0.642**	0.713**
	(3.47)	(6.82)	(3.14)	(3.17)
Resources	0.0132	0.00697	0.0243	0.0415
	(0.41)	(0.32)	(1.09)	(1.49)
lnGrowth	-0.0462	-0.0452	-0.320	-0.381
	(-0.18)	(-0.18)	(-1.18)	(-1.22)
Polity	0.192**	0.158***	0.130	-0.0307
	(3.09)	(3.80)	(1.90)	(-0.29)
OECD membership		0.420		-0.141
		(0.67)		(-0.16)
Constant	-27.03	-22.40***	-22.09***	-26.75***
	(-1.64)	(-3.53)	(-3.74)	(-3.41)
/mills				
lambda	0.329	0.192		
	(0.27)	(0.23)		
Observations	148	148	148	148

t statistics in parentheses
$*p < 0.05$, $**p < 0.01$, $***p < 0.001$

While logit, regression, and Heckman analysis support the hypothesis, as discussed before, lower levels of perceived corruption by the firms do not directly measure the political influence of these firms. The reason why the firms do not perceive corruption might be due to the low level of corruption in the country. Therefore, following the above analysis, I have run the same series of analyses with the other explanatory variables: *real corruption perception of the firms* and *real corruption perception of firms2*.[42] The results of the analysis are presented in Table 4.7 through Table 4.9.

---

42 These two variables are the independent variables which represent the corruption perception of firms based on the real level of corruption perception in a country.

Table 4.7. Logit Analysis of Whether Aid Is Given

	Model 9	**Model 10**
Real Corruption Perception of Firms	−0.0546*	
	(−1.97)	
lnGDP	2.940**	2.951**
	(2.89)	(2.90)
lnPopulation	1.208**	1.244**
	(2.92)	(2.93)
WTO membership	−2.472	−2.498
	(−1.18)	(−1.19)
Resources	0.0473	0.0489
	(0.87)	(0.89)
lnGrowth	−0.733	−0.715
	(−1.31)	(−1.27)
Polity	−0.0915	−0.0834
	(−0.49)	(−0.42)
OECD membership	−0.601	−0.355
	(−0.41)	(−0.24)
Neopatrimonial	9.518*	9.287
	(2.02)	(1.94)
Real Corruption Perception of Firms2		−0.0583*
		(−2.04)
Constant	−50.07***	50.78***
	(−3.33)	(−3.32)
Observations	148	148
Pseudo R^2	0.573	0.581

t statistics in parentheses
*$p < 0.05$, **$p < 0.01$, ***$p < 0.001$

In Models 9 and 10, firms' perception of corruption is also measured depending on the countries' level of corruption. In both models, the perception of corruption variables (Real corruption perception of firms and Real corruption perception of firms2) are still significant with negative coefficients. This suggests that the illiberal and autocratic regimes with a high level of perception of corruption relative to the real level of corruption in the country are more likely to be donors.

While Model 11 does not support the hypothesis, Model 12 supports the hypothesis with different measurements of the political influence of business elites. In both models, the perception of corruption by firms are estimated

Table 4.8. OLS Analysis of Amount of Given Aid

	Model 11	Model 12
Real Corruption Perception of Firms	−0.00897	
	(−1.89)	
lnGDP	0.390***	0.393***
	(3.46)	(3.50)
lnPopulation	0.342***	0.344***
	(4.44)	(4.47)
WTO membership	0.0581	0.0585
	(0.19)	(0.19)
Resources	0.00158	0.00140
	(0.14)	(0.13)
lnGrowth	−0.192	0.190
	(1.18)	(−1.17)
Polity	−0.0186	−0.0169
	(0.69)	(−0.63)
OECD membership	2.526***	2.555***
	(4.29)	(4.35)
Neopatrimonial	0.572	0.514
	(0.94)	(0.85)
Real Corruption Perception of Firms2		−0.00942*
		(−2.00)
Constant	−8.238***	−8.278***
	(−5.11)	(−5.14)
Observations	148	148
Adjusted R^2	0.341	0.343

t statistics in parentheses
$*p < 0.05$, $**p < 0.01$, $***p < 0.001$

relative to the level of corruption in the country. The regression analyses of Model 12 with real corruption perception of firms (2) support the hypothesis that autocratic and illiberal countries with a high political influence of export-oriented business elites are more likely to provide a higher amount of foreign assistance.

Models 13 and 14 are the Heckman analysis of logit and OLS analysis with different measurements of the political influence of business elites in order to ensure there are no potential biases in the OLS estimates. However, the Heckman analyses also show similar results suggesting that both aid giving and the amount of foreign assistance are influenced by the political influence of business elites.

Table 4.9. Heckman Analysis of Donorship and Amount of Given Aid

	Model 13: Amount of Given Aid	Model 14: Amount of Given Aid	Model 13: Is Aid Given	Model 14: Is Aid Given
Real Corruption Perception of Firms	−0.0340**		−0.0327*	
	(−2.68)		(−2.06)	
lnGDP	0.488	0.530	1.520**	1.552**
	(1.27)	(1.56)	(2.89)	(2.91)
lnPopulation	1.102***	1.124***	0.649**	0.683**
	(7.55)	(8.28)	(3.16)	(3.17)
Resources	0.0137	0.00989	0.0344	0.0337
	(0.55)	(0.48)	(1.28)	(1.23)
lnGrowth	−0.0557	−0.0704	−0.359	−0.362
	(−0.22)	(−0.31)	(−1.17)	(−1.16)
Polity	0.186***	0.174***	−0.0387	−0.0329
	(3.54)	(4.41)	(−0.39)	(−0.32)
OECD membership	0.243	0.480	−0.0969	0.190
	(0.34)	(0.89)	(−0.11)	(0.02)
WTO membership			−1.423	−1.465
			(−1.26)	(−1.27)
Neopatrimonial			5.232*	5.115*
			(2.07)	(1.99)
Real Corruption Perception of Firms2		−0.0337**		−0.0351*
		(−3.11)		(−2.15)
Constant	−19.35***	−20.23***	−26.63***	−27.45**
	(−3.37)	(−3.84)	(−3.52)	(−3.50)
/mills				
lambda	−0.454	−0.268		
	(−0.50)	(−0.38)		
Observations	148	148	148	148

t statistics in parentheses
*$p < 0.05$, **$p < 0.01$, ***$p < 0.001$

To better understand the substantive effect of the political influence of business elites on aid giving, I also computed the predicted probabilities of giving aid when holding all of the explanatory variables at means. The predicted probabilities can be seen in Figure 4.3 and Figure 4.4.

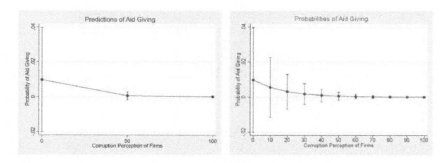

Figure 4.3. Predicted Probabilities of Aid Giving by Political Influence of Business

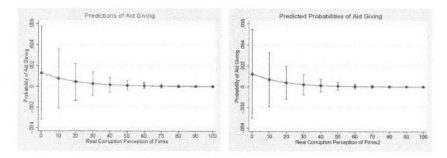

Figure 4.4. Predicted Probabilities of Aid Giving by Different Measures of Political Influence of Businesses and Real Level of Political Corruption

Based on these results, the probability of aid giving is higher when the corruption perception of export-oriented firms is lower. More specifically, when the business elites do not perceive corruption even if there is a certain level of political corruption and public sector corruption in the country, the autocratic and illiberal governments are more likely to provide foreign assistance.

4.4.1. Robustness Checks

Based on the primary findings of this research, it is clear that countries with high political influence from the export-oriented business elites are more likely to provide foreign assistance and more likely to provide a higher amount of assistance. This relationship has been tested through logit, OLS, and Heckman Selection analysis. However, testing whether these findings are robust and

Table 4.10. Probit Analysis of Whether Aid Is Given

	Model 15	Model 16
Corruption Perception of Firms	−0.0343*	−0.0351*
	(−2.23)	(−2.13)
lnGDP	1.388**	1.570**
	(3.24)	(2.85)
lnPopulation	0.642**	0.713**
	(3.14)	(3.17)
WTO membership	−1.499	−1.322
	(−1.52)	(−1.18)
Resources	0.0243	0.0415
	(1.09)	(1.49)
lnGrowth	−0.320	−0.381
	(−1.18)	(−1.22)
Polity	0.130	−0.0307
	(1.90)	(−0.29)
OECD membership		−0.141
		(−0.16)
Neopatrimonial		4.605
		(1.82)
Constant	−22.09***	−26.75***
	(−3.74)	(−3.41)
Observations	148	148
Pseudo R^2	0.529	0.585

t statistics in parentheses
*$p < 0.05$, **$p < 0.01$, ***$p < 0.001$

accurate is still crucial. To understand this, I employ additional tests for both binary dependent variable (aid giving) and continuous dependent variables (aid amount). Additionally, I measure the aid amount as a share of GNI in addition to the single aid amount value. Table 4.10 illustrates the results of probit analysis to check the robustness of the logit analysis with the donorship variable as dependent, and the corruption perception of firms as independent variables. Table 4.11 presents the results of probit analysis with the donorship variable as dependent, and real corruption perception of firms as independent variables.

As seen in the results of the probit analysis, the results of the logit analysis have not changed. The firms' perception of corruption is still negatively associated with the donorship variable.

Table 4.11. Probit Analysis of Whether Aid Is Given

	Model 17	Model 18
Real Corruption Perception of Firms	−0.0327* (−2.06)	
lnGDP	1.520** (2.89)	1.552** (2.91)
lnPopulation	0.649** (3.16)	0.683** (3.17)
WTO membership	−1.423 (−1.26)	−1.465 (−1.27)
Resources	0.0344 (1.28)	0.0337 (1.23)
lnGrowth	−0.359 (−1.17)	−0.362 (−1.16)
Polity	−0.0387 (−0.39)	−0.0329 (−0.32)
OECD membership	−0.0969 (−0.11)	0.0190 (0.02)
Neopatrimonial	5.232 * (2.07)	5.115* (1.99)
Real Corruption Perception of Firms2		−0.0351* (−2.15)
Constant	−26.63*** (−3.52)	−27.45*** (−3.50)
Observations	148	148
Pseudo R^2	0.575	0.584

t statistics in parentheses
*$p < 0.05$, **$p < 0.01$, ***$p < 0.001$

Following the probit analysis, I check the robustness of OLS analysis findings with the Tobit analysis. As discussed in the Heckman analysis section, the dependent variable is bounded by 0 and cannot take any non-negative values; therefore, it is essential to avoid any potential bias. Table 4.12 illustrates the results of probit analysis to check the robustness of the OLS analysis with the aid amount variable as dependent, and corruption perception of firms as independent variables. Table 4.13 presents the results of Tobit analysis with the aid amount variable as dependent, and real corruption perception of firms as independent variables.

Table 4.12. Tobit Analysis of Amount of Given Aid

	Model 19	Model 20
lnAid		
Corruption Perception of Firms	-0.164*	-0.152*
	(-2.35)	(-2.28)
lnGDP	6.412**	6.940**
	(3.23)	(2.82)
lnPopulation	3.484**	3.580***
	(3.33)	(3.37)
WTO membership	-6.820	-5.808
	(-1.47)	(-1.18)
Resources	0.106	0.169
	(0.98)	(1.38)
lnGrowth	-1.658	-1.612
	(-1.31)	(-1.26)
Polity	0.608*	-0.0568
	(2.02)	(-0.14)
OECD membership		-1.242
		(-0.38)
Neopatrimonial		19.20
		(1.90)
Constant	-110.3***	-124.9**
	(-3.66)	(-3.35)
/		
var(e.lnAid)	24.24*	20.49*
	(2.10)	(2.12)
Observations	148	148
Pseudo R^2	0.336	0.370

t statistics in parentheses
*$p < 0.05$, **$p < 0.01$, ***$p < 0.001$

Table 4.12 is the robustness test of the OLS regression on aid amount with corruption perception of export-oriented firms variable via Tobit analysis. Both Model 19 and Model 20, with additional control variables, support the OLS findings that higher political influence (lower level of corruption perception) results in a high amount of foreign assistance by non-democratic countries. Table 4.13 presents the results of Tobit analysis with the real corruption perception of firms variable. These variables are also significant in the robustness test with Tobit analysis.

As the last test, I examine the potential impact of the political influence of business elites on the generosity of non-democratic and illiberal donors. This

Table 4.13. Tobit Analysis of Amount of Given Aid

	Model 21	Model 22
Real Corruption Perception of Firms	−0.149* (−2.16)	
lnGDP	6.961** (2.82)	6.916 ** (2.86)
lnPopulation	3.429** (3.30)	3.496** (3.35)
WTO membership	−6.204 (−1.20)	−6.422 (−1.25)
Resources	0.150 (1.20)	0.140 (1.15)
lnGrowth	−1.542 (−1.19)	−1.545 (−1.21)
Polity	−0.126 (−0.32)	−0.0806 (−0.21)
OECD membership	−0.996 (−0.30)	−0.500 (−0.16)
Neopatrimonial	23.16* (2.14)	21.81* (2.09)
Real Corruption Perception of Firms2		−0.154* (−2.28)
Constant	−129.3** (−3.36)	−129.3*** (−3.40)
/		
var(e.lnAid)	21.61* (2.11)	20.68* (2.12)
Observations	148	148
Pseudo R^2	0.364	0.370

t statistics in parentheses
*$p < 0.05$, **$p < 0.01$, ***$p < 0.001$

can also be seen as a sensitivity check of the aid amount variable because it is a different measure of the given aid amount. The results can be seen in Table 4.14.

Table 4.14 represents the Tobit analysis of the generosity of the donors by including another measure of the political influence of export-oriented firms. Both corruption perception and real corruption perception2 measures have a significant effect on aid amount as a share of the countries' GNI, although the impact of these variables is very small.

Table 4.14. Tobit Analysis of Generosity

	Model 23	Model 24	Model 25
aid as a share			
Corruption Perception of Firms	−0.0000389*		
	(−2.34)		
lnGDP	0.00141*	0.00140*	0.00140*
	(2.39)	(2.40)	(2.40)
lnPopulation	0.000693**	0.000656**	0.000656**
	(2.74)	(2.68)	(2.68)
lnGrowth	−0.000230	−0.000217	−0.000217
	(−0.75)	(−0.70)	(−0.70)
WTO membership	−0.00180	−0.00191	−0.00191
	(−1.54)	(−1.55)	(−1.55)
Resources	0.0000324	0.0000278	0.0000278
	(1.19)	(1.02)	(1.02)
Polity	0.0000736	0.0000567	0.0000567
	(0.78)	(0.60)	(0.60)
OECD membership	0.000370	0.000434	0.000434
	(0.47)	(0.56)	(0.56)
Neopatrimonial	0.00300	0.00402	0.00402
	(1.36)	(1.71)	(1.71)
Real Corruption Perception of Firms2		−0.0000391*	−0.0000391*
		(−2.26)	(−2.26)
Constant	−0.0244**	−0.0254**	−0.0254**
	(−2.79)	(−2.85)	(−2.85)
/			
var(e.aidasashare)	0.00000112*	0.00000114*	0.00000114*
	(2.19)	(2.18)	(2.18)
Observations	148	148	148
Pseudo R^2	−0.821	−0.812	−0.812

t statistics in parentheses
*$p < 0.05$, **$p < 0.01$, ***$p < 0.001$

Chapter 5 Donor Preferences in Illiberal and Autocratic Regimes

Abstract: What influences the aid preferences of the non-democratic or illiberal donor countries? This chapter of the book examines the theoretical argument on whether the business-elite configuration in non-democratic and illiberal donors influences the aid preferences of the governments, such as the number of low and high amount of projects, the sectoral distribution, and the type of recipient. Using data from AidData and the World Bank, the hypotheses are tested through regression analysis.

Keywords: Sectoral Distribution of Foreign Aid, Aid Recipients, Elite Configuration, Aid Projects

5.1. Introduction

This book analyzes foreign aid policies of non-democratic and illiberal donors in two aspects: motivation and preferences. The fourth chapter of this book focused on the *motivation* of these donors and found that donors with autocratic and illiberal regime types are driven by the political influence of business elites in their aid giving as well as the amount of aid provided. After examining the motivation of non-democratic donors in chapter four, this chapter turns to the *preferences* of non-democratic donors in their aid policies. It analyzes three central hypotheses (Hypothesis 2, 3, and 4) regarding the autocratic and illiberal donors' preferences as complementary to chapter 4.

This chapter analyzes the relationship between business elites and the foreign aid preferences of non-democratic and illiberal donors. More specifically, the main argument of this chapter is that business-elite configuration in non-democratic and illiberal donors influences the aid preferences of the governments, as discussed in the theory chapter. With this focus, this chapter explains the methodology and tests used to examine the relationship between elite configuration and donor preferences that are discussed in chapter 3. The chapter starts with the data and data sources that are used for independent and dependent variables in the analyses. Then, the chapter continues with the estimation techniques used to test three main hypotheses to analyze the relationship between elite configuration and the preferences of the donors. Following the estimation strategies, results will be discussed and the chapter will be concluded with the robustness tests.

5.2. Data

In line with the theory I suggest in chapter 3, I test the relationship between business-elite configuration in authoritarian and illiberal regimes and the preferences on their aid allocation. Analyzing this relationship, I define the dependent variables as measures of the different kinds of aid preferences: *the value of the aid projects, sector of aid projects,* and *types of recipients of the aid projects.* The primary independent variable is the measure of *business-elite configuration* and is described as the level of competition among the business elites in the donor country. A detailed list of the variables used in this analysis can be seen in Table 5.1.

5.2.1. Dependent Variables

Aid Preferences: Value of the Foreign Aid

In this chapter, I aim to test three groups of hypotheses in order to show how aid preferences of non-democracies are influenced by the configuration of business elites, more specifically, the level of competition among the industry and market. Based on these three main hypotheses, I propose three main preferences of donor countries. The first one is the *value of the projects.* As is discussed in chapter 3, theoretically, I expect that when there is a high level of competition among the business elites, the leader of the country takes into account this competition and distributes economic resources among the business elites accordingly in order to keep the business elites loyal. Moreover, high level of competition still signals that there might be a challenge against the rule of the leader. Being aware of that, the leader gives incentives to share the resources similarly rather than channeling the opportunities to the dominant elites and ignoring the others. In line with that, the leader needs to distribute the resources among the business elites. When there is more competition, the leader needs to provide opportunities for more diverse business elites, which, I argue, is reflected in the number of aid projects. Therefore, I expect that non-democratic governments with a higher level of competition among the business elites are more likely to provide a higher number of low-value projects than the ones with a lower level of competition among the business elites.

Similarly, when there is dominance in the business-elite configuration, the leader needs to provide opportunities for this dominant group. This is also translated to the aid values, and the non-democratic governments with more dominance in their business-elite configuration are more likely to provide a higher number of high-value assistance. Relying on that, to test these hypotheses, I use *the number of projects with a smaller amount* as one of the dependent variables and *the number of projects with a higher amount* as another one of the dependent variables of my hypotheses.

The first group of dependent variables, which are the number of high and low amount of projects, come from the AidData, Research Release 3.1 thin version (AidData, 2017a) and AidData Global Chinese Official Finance Dataset v1 (AidData, 2017b). As explained in the previous empirical chapter, AidData has project-level foreign assistance data covering most new donors, including non-democratic donors. In this AidData's Research Release aid database, there is a version that covers donor/recipient aggregated aid data and provides foreign aid data between 1947 and 2013 for 96 donors, summing up the yearly dyadic level aid activities rather than providing project-level assistance. Because I am interested in the number of the high and low amount of projects in a year, I use the donor/recipient aggregated version for arranging the dyadic level aid activities in a given year.

However, the Research Release database of AidData does not cover Chinese foreign assistance extensively since AidData has a separate database for Chinese assistance. To solve the issue, I merge AidData's Global Chinese Official Finance Dataset, 2000–2014, Version 1 database with the Research Release 3.1 databases. This Chinese database covers the Chinese official assistance between the years of 2000 and 2014 and suggests information for 4,373 projects.

Notwithstanding, these databases do not have a variable regarding the number of low and high amount of projects. To figure out the number of the high and low amount of projects, I benefit from the thin release of AidData and calculate the number of the high and low amount of projects in two phases: First, I find the mean amount of the total number of projects in the thin release, including all the donors' project-level activities. The mean amount of projects in the entire dataset is 451,1247 dollars. Based on this mean amount, I identify the projects that are higher than the mean amount and lower than the mean amount, and code them as low-amount projects and high-amount projects consecutively. Following that, I count how many numbers of a high and low amount of projects the donor country provided for each recipient in a year. As a result, I create two dependent variables as the number of high amount of projects and number of low amount of projects in a given year for each recipient country to test the impact of competition among the elites on the aid-value preference.

Aid Preferences: Aid Sector

The second preference of the donor countries is related to their foreign aid sector. While theoretically, countries need to provide assistance in the sector that can strengthen the recipient countries' resources or services, in practice, donor countries also need to calculate which sectors these donors provide assistance to serve for their interests. If the country has no resources in the sector that is needed by the recipient, then donor country cannot provide assistance in this sector. Also, some sectors might be more advantageous for donors than others. Particularly in non-democratic countries where the importance of business elites is higher due to the reason that they take parts in the leaders' supporting coalition, the leaders provide assistance in the sector that can benefit the business elites. Following this theoretical background, I expect that if there is a dominant sector in the non-democratic countries' market, then the aid sector will also be influenced by that, and this dominant sector will also be reflected in the donors' preferred foreign aid sector. Therefore, in the second hypothesis, I analyze if the elite configuration, more specifically, the level of competition among the business elites is also reflected in the sectoral distribution of foreign assistance.

To analyze this relationship, I identify the dependent variable as *the level of sectoral dominance/variation in the aid projects*. To obtain this dependent variable, I again rely on AidData database. AidData's Donor/Recipient/Year/ Purpose aggregated release has a "purpose of the aid" variable which identifies the sector of the assistance. However, this database is also project-level data; therefore, I assign codes for each of the purpose/sector and calculate the number of projects in each sector in a given year in a dyadic level. Accordingly, I categorize the Health, Education, Government, Civil Society, Water, Security and Conflict variables as social infrastructure, road transport, air transport, energy (including gas and oil), electricity, urban and rural development sectors as economic infrastructure, fishing, forestry, and all agriculture-related variables as agriculture, fishing and forestry category, all industry related projects, mining, mineral, construction (including site preservation), trade, international trade agreement, export and import support projects as industry category. Besides, I categorize all food assistance including basic nutrition assistance, reconstruction, relief and rehabilitation and budget relief assistance as emergency category and multisector assistance and assistance in which sectors are not identified as other and multisector category.

As a result, I calculate the number of projects for each sector. Nonetheless, the number of projects in each sector alone does not provide any information regarding the sectoral variation. Therefore, I employ the Herfindahl Hirschman

Index's formula (Rhoades, 1993) to calculate the variation in the provided aid sectors. Relying on the Herfindahl Index's formula, first, I take the percentages of these numbers of projects for each sector relative to the total number of projects in a given dyad-year. Then, take the square of these percentages and sum them up. As a consequence, I obtain my dependent variable, which is the level of sectoral variation, in the provided foreign assistance in a given dyad-year.

Aid Preferences: Type of Recipient

Donors countries also need to decide which countries they will provide aid to. Therefore, the third preference of the donor countries is defined as the selection of the recipient countries. Leaders of the donor countries need to select their recipients strategically, even when their main purpose is helping out the other countries. They need to select their recipients strategically so that the entire aid policy can also help the leader to maintain his power. Because foreign aid also benefits the leader by bringing some support from the business elites in exchange of providing some aid project contracts and trade opportunities to the business elites, then the recipient countries of foreign aid must be the countries that work best for the business elites' interests. In this bargaining process, the business-elite structure influences the selection of the recipient countries in such a way that can work for the business elites' interests. Therefore, the type of recipients depends on the business-elite structure. If there is a dominance in the business-elite configuration, which translates that one group of business elites are more dominant, then that implies there is not much competition among the donor countries' dominant elite groups, and these dominant elite group is more likely to be in the supporting coalition of the leader. Since the leader needs to provide opportunities for this dominant business-elite group, the leader needs to provide assistance to the countries which work best for the business elites' interests. When there is less competition in the business-elite configuration, the leaders in the non-democracies provide assistance to the resource-rich or higher-level income group countries so that this can pave the way for trade opportunities on behalf of the dominant business elites.

As a result, it can be expected that when there is less competition in the business-elite structure, foreign aid is provided to the higher-income countries, as argued. To test the hypothesis, the dependent variable is defined as *the type of recipient* and measured by the type of recipient. I use two different measures as a type of recipient variable. The first one is the income group of the recipient, and the second is the level of total natural resources of the recipient as a share of its GDP.

Both measures of the type of recipient come from the World Bank database (World Bank, 2019a, 2018d). The first type of recipient variable is the income group classification of the World Bank. Accordingly, there are four groups of countries based on their income, which are low-income, low-middle-income, upper-middle income, and high-income group. Therefore, this variable is an ordinal variable about whether the aid is given to the higher-income group countries than the others and coded from 1 to 4 in an ascending income level order. The second variable, on the other hand, is the total natural resources as a percentage of the GDP variable. World Bank data gives information about the total natural resources rents of the country as a share of its GDP as a continuous variable.

5.2.2. Independent Variables

I use one primary independent variable in all hypotheses testing in this chapter. In all of the hypotheses regarding the aid preferences of non-democratic and illiberal donors, it is tested that configuration of the business elites would influence the aid preferences of governments with autocratic and illiberal regimes. Based on that, the primary independent variable is defined as the export-oriented business-elite configuration in terms of business elites' diversification and dominance.

Measuring Configuration of Business Elites and the Herfindahl Hirschman Index

Because the aim of the book is analyzing the influence of the configuration of business elites and particularly the export-oriented business elite, we need to determine a valid measure for this elite configuration. Furthermore, in terms of elite configuration, the focus of this chapter is the competition among the export-oriented business elites.

One common measure of the level of market competition is the Herfindahl Hirschman Index (HHI) since it calculates the level of market concentration based on the share of each market. As is presented in the formula below, HHI is calculated by squaring the market shares of all firms in a market and then summing the squares. MS_i denotes the market share of each firm i for the n number of firms in the market (Rhoades, 1993).

$$HHI = \sum_{i=1}^{n} \left(MS_i \right)^2$$

Therefore, in order to measure the distribution in business elite's configuration in terms of the level of competition among export-oriented business elites, I use the HHI. I obtain the data of HHI for each donor from the World Bank, IBRD-IDA database. The World Bank defines HHI as "a measure of the dispersion of trade value across an exporter's partners" (World Bank, 2019b).

Accordingly, if a country's trade is concentrated in very few markets, it is highly concentrated; in other words, there is dominance in the market. Therefore, the index value will be very close to the highest value, which is 1. Likewise, if a country's trade is not highly concentrated, and is diversified, the value of the index will be close to the lowest value, which is 0. To sum up, the independent variable is a continuous measure of the market concentration between the value of 0 and 1 from the lowest concentration to the highest concentration.

5.2.3. Control Variables

In order to test the relationship between concentration in the configuration of business elites and foreign assistance preferences of the non-democratic and illiberal countries, I include some of the control variables to measure donor motivation as I used in chapter 4. To be more specific, these variables are a log of GDP per capita and log of the population from the World Bank's database (World Bank, 2018a, 2018b), OECD membership from the OECD's website (OECD, 2019e), and WTO/GATT membership from the WTO's website (WTO, 2019).

It is essential to include the donor's GDP variable because a donor's GDP might have an impact on the donor's preferences, especially on the number of the high and low amount of projects. Donors' population is also considered to have an impact on the amount of assistance provided; therefore, it can also affect the number of high and low number of projects. OECD membership might have an impact on the donors' preferences since OECD suggests some criteria in terms of recipient selection and aid sector selection and puts some pressure for following these criteria on the member donor governments. Being a WTO member is also a significant variable to include in the analyses since more trade-oriented countries might be more likely to provide assistance. The GDP and population variables are used as the log version, which are both continuous level of measurements. Both OECD membership and WTO membership variables are binary variables and coded as 1 for being a member in a given dyad-year and 0 for not being a member in a given dyad-year.

In addition to the donor's GDP and population, I included recipient's GDP and population as control variables, given that the unit of analysis is dyad-year in the analyses of this chapter. Controlling recipient GDP and population might be useful to isolate the influence of these variables on the aid preferences of the donors. I also included the recipient's WTO membership as another control variable. Similar to the variables of donors' GDP, population, and WTO membership, both the population, and recipients' GDP are used as the log versions and as the continuous level of measurements. On the other hand, the variable of OECD membership is used as a binary measurement that is coded 1 for being a member and 0 for not being a member.

Besides these control variables that are similarly used in chapter 4, I include additional control variables since I am interested in the preferences of donors at the dyadic level rather than focusing on the country-year donor motivation. In dyad-year level data, where there are both donors and recipients, inter-relationships between the dyadic countries also matter. Therefore, I include the contiguity, alliances, and Cold War variables to control the potential impact of distance and closeness on aid relationships between dyads. Both contiguity and alliance variables are obtained from the Correlates of War Project database (Stinnet et al., 2002; Correlates of War Project, 2016). The contiguity variable is an ordinal measure of the COW Direct Contiguity v3.2 database and is coded between 0 and 5. COW defines land contiguity as "the intersection of the homeland territory of the two states in the dyad, either through a land boundary or a river (such as the Rio Grande in the case of the US-Mexico border)" whereas it offers four different categories for the water contiguity based on a separation by the water of 12, 24, 150, and 400 miles. Code 0 represents no contiguity between the dyads in a given year. Code 1 is for the land contiguity, whereas the higher values between codes 2 and 4 represent separation by the higher miles in terms of water contiguity (Stinnet et al., 2002; Correlates of War Project, 2016).

Alliance variable is taken from the Formal Alliances v4.1 dataset of the COW project, which "records all formal alliances among states between 1816 and 2012, including mutual defense pacts, nonaggression treaties, and ententes" (Gibler, 2009; Singer & Small, 1966; Correlates of War Project, 2013). If the dyads have alliances, the variable is coded as 1, and if there are no alliances between the dyads in a given year, then the variable is coded as 0 (Correlates of War Project, 2013). Cold War control variable is also coded as binary. Code 1 is assigned if foreign aid is given in the Cold War era, and code 0 is assigned if foreign aid is not provided in the Cold War era. Below is Table 5.1, which presents the details for the variables used in the statistical models.

Table 5.1. Variable Names, Operationalizations, Sources, and Original Variable Name

Variable Names	Operationalizations	Sources
High-Amount Projects	Number of High-Amount projects in a given dyad-year	AidData (2017a, 2017b)
Low Amount Projects	Number of Low Amount projects in a given dyad-year	AidData (2017a, 2017b)
Aid Sector Concentration	Diversification in the aid sector that is given in a dyad-year. Calculated based on the Herfindahl market concentration index (HHI). Continuous measure between 0 and 1.	AidData (2017a, 2017b), World Bank (2019b)
Type of Recipients	Recipient countries income group. 1 the recipient is low income 2 the recipient is low-middle income 3 the recipient is upper-middle income 4 the recipient is high income	World Bank (2019a)
Market Concentration	Herfindahl Hirschman Index (HHI): a measure of the dispersion of trade value across an exporter's partners. Continuous measure between 0 and 1.	World Bank (2019b)
lnGDP_d	Natural log of donor's gross domestic product per capita in U.S. million dollars at current prices.	World Bank (2018a)
lnGDP_r	Natural log of recipient's gross domestic product per capita in U.S. million dollars at current prices.	World Bank (2018a)
lnPopulation_d	Natural log of the population of a donor country in a given dyad-year.	World Bank (2018b)

(*Continued*)

Table 5.1. Continued

Variable Names	Operationalizations	Sources
lnPopulation_r	Natural log of the population of a donor country in a given dyad-year.	World Bank (2018b)
WTO membership_d	Is donor country a WTO member? If a donor country is a WTO member in a given dyad-year. 0 not a WTO member in a given year 1 a WTO member in a given year	WTO (2019)
WTO membership_r	Is recipient country a WTO member? If a recipient country is a WTO member in a given dyad-year. 0 not a WTO member in a given year 1 a WTO member in a given year	WTO (2019)
Contiguity	Are dyads contiguous in a given dyad-year? 0 not contiguous 1 land contiguous 4 is water contiguous	Correlates of War (2016)
Alliance	Is there an alliance between donor and recipient in a given dyad-year? Status of an alliance between donor and recipient in a given dyad-year 0 not alliance 1 alliance	Correlates of War (2013)
OECD membership_d	Is donor country an OECD member? If a donor country is an OECD member in a given dyad-year. 0 not an OECD member in a given year 1 an OECD member in a given year	OECD (2019e)

Table 5.1. Continued

Variable Names	Operationalizations	Sources
Cold War	Is aid project provided during in Cold War era? If aid project is provided during the Cold War. 0 not Cold War 1 Cold War	

5.3. Estimation Strategy and Tests

In order to test the hypotheses on the relationship between the business-elite configuration and donors' foreign aid preferences, I had to employ several strategies. These strategies include creating a dataset by merging different databases, collecting data, matching the variables from different databases, recoding and transforming variables, employing the proper tests, and checking the results with additional robustness tests.

First, I have created a dyad-year dataset by merging two datasets from AidData, as explained in the previous chapter. Since AidData provides project-level data, I had to reconfigure this database for the dyad-year by summing the amount and number of projects for each donor and recipient in a given year. After I have created the dyad-year dataset based on two databases from AidData, I had to filter out the liberal democratic donors from the dataset. For this step, I have followed the same procedure as I did in chapter 4. Essentially, I have filtered out the countries with liberal democratic regime types from the database based on the V-Dem's "regimes of the world (v2x_regime) variable" for the same reasons as I did in chapter 4. As a result, I have obtained a dyadic dataset of donors and recipients with 4,644 observations between 1962 and 2014.

After I have gathered the main dataset with a dyad-year unit of analysis with the aid amount variables, I have created a "number of high and low-value projects" variables. To do so, first, I have taken the mean of all of the projects amounts in the entire AidData Core Research Release dataset. Based on this mean amount, I have considered the projects lower than the mean as low-value projects and the ones that are higher than the mean as high amount of projects. Then, I have counted the high and low-value projects for each dyad-year and code them accordingly.

For the second dependent variable, which is variation among the aid sector, I have followed a highly similar procedure. I have coded the sector of the projects based on the sector classification of OECD. As a result, I have obtained six main groups of sectors: social infrastructure, economic infrastructure, agriculture, forestry and fishing, industry, other assistance and humanitarian (emergency and food) assistance. After I have counted the number of projects in each sector in a given dyad-year, I have assigned codes based on this number. Then, I have applied Herfindahl's Market Concentration Index formula to aid sector data. Relying on this formula, I have calculated the sectoral variation in the provided assistance by taking the share of each type of aid sector, squaring them, and summing the results. Consequently, I have obtained an aid sector concentration index. For the third dependent variable, I have gathered the data on the recipient's income group from the World Bank, matched the data with my dataset, and recoded them from 1 to 4, indicating that higher values are associated with higher-income groups.

For the rest of the variables, including the HHI, not much work has been required except gathering them from the different databases and matching them with my dyad-year database. I have taken the log of the donors' GDP, recipients' GDP, donors' population, recipients' population, and total natural resources of recipient variables. The descriptive statistics of the variables are presented in Table 5.2 below.

Table 5.2. Descriptive Statistics

variable	count	mean	sd	min	max
High-Amount Projects	4,186	.6856187	.9948823	0	15
Low Amount Projects	4,186	1.406355	3.839796	0	83
Aid Sector Concentration	3,973	.8331744	.2473516	.2	1
Type of Recipients	3,204	1.832709	.8078471	1	4
Market Concentration	2,649	.0813817	.0264828	.04	.28
lnGDP_d	3,486	27.28335	1.561173	24.50393	29.75128
lnGDP_r	3,680	23.3446	1.910301	17.20647	30.34276
lnPopulation_d	3,817	17.60327	2.688848	12.71518	21.03389
lnPopulation_r	3,960	15.79675	1.951152	9.195937	21.02882
WTO membership_d	4,161	.8137467	.3893577	0	1
WTO membership_r	3,991	.6852919	.4644577	0	1
Contiguity	4,053	.161362	.6870091	0	5
Alliance	3,799	.2026849	.4020526	0	1
OECD membership_d	4,161	.0684932	.2526206	0	1
Cold War	4,172	.2145254	.4105419	0	1

5.4. Results

To analyze the impact of business-elite configuration on the foreign aid preferences of the non-democratic donors, I use different types of tests. Since I have three separate hypotheses to analyze the foreign aid preferences, and each dependent variable in each hypothesis has a different level of measurement, I employ different types of tests such as OLS, negative binomial regression analysis, Tobit, and ordinal logit (ologit) analysis.

In the first hypothesis, I intend to test the relationship between the level of competition in donors' market and the number of the high and low amount of projects in a given year. Since the dependent variables, a number of the high amount of projects and a number of the low amount of projects, are continuous variables, I use linear regression. However, both the number of a high amount of projects and the number of a low amount of projects variables are count variables that are bounded with 0, which means there is no value below 0. When the count variable has 0 as a common value, linear regression modeling can be a simplification and may come with biases. In order to avoid simplification and increase the accuracy of the model, I also use negative binomial regression.

The first model is the OLS regression on a high amount of projects provided. The second, third, and fourth models include additional control variables in the OLS analysis to see whether they will change the estimates. The results of these models are presented in Table 5.3.

Table 5.3. OLS Analysis of Aid Projects Values

	Model 1	Model 2	Model 3	Model 4
Market Concentration	3.959***	4.106***	4.158***	3.634***
	(4.38)	(4.56)	(4.75)	(3.99)
lnGDP_d	0.0989***	0.279***	0.237***	0.226***
	(6.07)	(5.70)	(4.59)	(4.36)
lnGDP_r	−0.00743	−0.142***	0.152***	−0.144***
	(−0.60)	(−6.76)	(−6.76)	(−6.39)
lnPopulation_d		−0.120***	−0.0908**	−0.0866**
		(−4.02)	(−3.00)	(−2.85)
lnPopulation_r		0.162***	0.169***	0.171***
		(7.73)	(7.65)	(7.71)
Contiguity			0.0661	0.0629
			(1.90)	(1.82)

(Continued)

Table 5.3. Continued

	Model 1	Model 2	Model 3	Model 4
Alliance			0.0156	0.0233
			(0.24)	(0.36)
OECD Membership_d				−0.491*
				(−2.39)
WTO Membership_d				−0.171
				(−1.70)
WTO Membership_r				−0.202***
				(−3.77)
Cold War				−0.0186
				(−0.33)
Constant	−2.211***	−4.393***	−3.678***	−3.321***
	(−3.66)	(−4.71)	(−3.72)	(−3.34)
Observations	2,441	2,441	2,201	2,195
Adjusted R^2	0.017	0.045	0.048	0.057

t statistics in parentheses
$*p < 0.05$, $**p < 0.01$, $***p < 0.001$

Table 5.3 shows the results on whether business-elite configuration influences the aid amount preferences. In Model 1, the main explanatory variable is market concentration. According to the theory of this book, the higher the dominance in the elite configuration, the higher number of high value of aid projects are provided. Looking at the results of the first analysis, we see that there is a positive correlation between the primary independent variable and dependent variable, supporting the hypothesis of the theory.

Model 2, Model 3, and Model 4 include additional control variables in order to test if the additional control variable would affect the results. However, the relationship between the level of competition within the business-elite configuration and the number of high-value aid projects is still significant in all models, even after including the variables such as population, membership to certain international organizations, and alliances.

Given that the dependent variable is the count variable, I re-test the models with the negative binomial regression analysis to capture more reliable results. Table 5.4 presents the replication of the results with the negative binomial analysis.

Table 5.4. Negative Binomial Analysis of Aid Projects Values

	Model 5	Model 6	Model 7	Model 8
High-amount project				
Market Concentration	5.966***	6.903***	6.881***	6.089***
	(5.16)	(5.75)	(5.73)	(4.92)
lnGDP_d	0.151***	0.490***	0.418***	0.402***
	(6.89)	(6.85)	(5.38)	(5.15)
lnGDP_r	–0.0143	–0.233***	–0.250***	–0.234***
	(–0.85)	(–7.95)	(–7.67)	(–7.15)
lnPopulation_d		–0.220***	–0.174***	–0.166***
		(–5.20)	(–3.87)	(–3.70)
lnPopulation_r		0.255***	0.268***	0.268***
		(8.80)	(8.45)	(8.43)
Contiguity			0.115*	0.103*
			(2.47)	(2.21)
Alliance			–0.0102	–0.0249
			(–0.11)	(–0.25)
WTO Membership_d				–0.237
				(–1.94)
WTO Membership_r				–0.296***
				(–4.21)
OECD Membership_d				–19.31
				(–0.00)
Cold War				–0.0249
				(–0.32)
Constant	–4.755***	–9.081***	–7.807***	–7.343***
	(–5.84)	(–6.69)	(–5.27)	(–4.95)
/				
lnalpha	–0.454***	–0.611***	–0.650***	–0.701***
	(–4.41)	(–5.53)	(–5.33)	(–5.61)
Observations	2,441	2,441	2,201	2,195
Pseudo R^2	0.011	0.029	0.030	0.039

t statistics in parentheses
$*p < 0.05$, $**p < 0.01$, $***p < 0.001$

In addition to the OLS analysis, negative binomial regression analysis also shows that an increase in the concentration of the market causes an increase in the number of high-value aid projects. The results of the negative binomial models are significant, supporting the hypothesis, even when the additional control variables are included in the model.

Although these models test the increase in the high-valued aid projects, the numbers of these projects do not account for the low-valued aid projects, given that the dependent variable only counts the high-valued aid projects. For that reason, I ran the OLS and negative binomial tests one more time but, this time, used the number of low-value projects as a dependent variable. Results of the OLS analysis with the number of low amount projects can be found in Table 5.5, whereas the results of the negative binomial analysis can be found in Table 5.6.

Table 5.5. OLS Analysis of Aid Projects Values

	Model 9	Model 10	Model 11	Model 12
Market Concentration	−26.65***	−26.19***	−27.13***	−23.64***
	(−8.05)	(−7.85)	(−8.00)	(−6.67)
lnGDP_d	−0.513***	−0.227	0.182	0.153
	(−8.61)	(−1.25)	(0.91)	(0.76)
lnGDP_r	0.181***	0.0638	−0.117	−0.143
	(3.99)	(0.82)	(−1.34)	(−1.63)
lnPopulation_d		−0.187	−0.338**	−0.315**
		(−1.70)	(−2.88)	(−2.66)
lnPopulation_r		0.139	0.326***	0.348***
		(1.79)	(3.80)	(4.03)
Contiguity			0.141	0.155
			(1.04)	(1.15)
Alliance			1.640***	1.685***
			(6.49)	(6.62)
OECD Membership_d				0.00714
				(0.01)
WTO Membership_d				1.454***
				(3.73)
WTO Membership_r				−0.0267
				(−0.13)
Cold War				−0.0390
				(−0.18)
Constant	14.12***	10.21**	2.808	1.794
	(6.40)	(2.95)	(0.73)	(0.46)
Observations	2,441	2,441	2,201	2,195
Adjusted R^2	0.051	0.052	0.075	0.078

t statistics in parentheses
$^*p < 0.05$, $^{**}p < 0.01$, $^{***}p < 0.001$

Table 5.6. Negative Binomial Analysis of Aid Projects Values

	Model 13	Model 14	Model 15	Model 16
Low amount project				
Market Concentration	−15.44***	−14.72***	−15.07***	−12.90***
	(−12.61)	(−11.99)	(−12.43)	(−10.30)
lnGDP_d	−0.290***	−0.117	0.0611	0.0593
	(−12.35)	(−1.85)	(0.91)	(0.89)
lnGDP_r	0.0987***	0.0325	−0.0369	−0.0574
	(5.80)	(1.12)	(−1.21)	(−1.90)
lnPopulation_d		−0.116**	−0.185***	−0.177***
		(−3.00)	(−4.66)	(−4.51)
lnPopulation_r		0.0791**	0.159***	0.176***
		(2.66)	(5.09)	(5.66)
Contiguity			0.124*	0.137*
			(2.31)	(2.56)
Alliance			0.668***	0.671***
			(8.33)	(8.49)
WTO Membership_d				1.760***
				(7.78)
WTO Membership_r				−0.0226
				(−0.30)
OECD Membership_d				0.142
				(0.55)
Cold War				−0.0284
				(−0.37)
Constant	7.530***	5.141***	1.727	−0.0212
	(8.79)	(4.16)	(1.31)	(−0.02)
/				
lnalpha	0.438***	0.425***	0.324***	0.263***
	(10.09)	(9.76)	(6.92)	(5.49)
Observations	2,441	2,441	2,201	2,195
Pseudo R^2	0.031	0.032	0.045	0.053

t statistics in parentheses
*$p < 0.05$, **$p < 0.01$, ***$p < 0.001$

While previous OLS and negative binomial regressions test the number of high-valued aid projects, the last models use both tests separately to test the number of low-value aid projects. In the previous tests, the results show that as the dominance among the business-elite configuration increases, the number of high-value projects increases. Likewise, but in a different way, the new results also support the hypothesis on the relationship between business-elite configuration and aid-projects value. As the results of OLS and negative binomial regression indicate, there is a negative relationship between the dependent and independent variables meaning that when the dominance in the elite configuration increases, the number of low-value projects decreases, supporting the hypothesis of the theory.

To better understand the substantive effect of the market concentration in the donors' business elite's structure on the value of the aid projects, I also computed the predicted margins of the number of high and low amount of projects. Figure 5.1 illustrates the predictive margins of high-value projects, whereas Figure 5.2 illustrates the predictive margins of low-value projects.

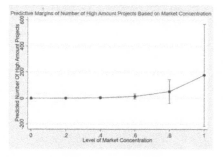

Figure 5.1. Predicted Margins of High-Value Aid Projects

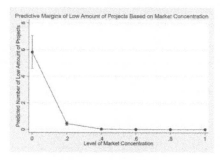

Figure 5.2. Predicted Margins of Low-Value Aid Projects

In the second hypothesis, I aim to analyze if the level of competition in the donor's market has an impact on the preferences of the donor in terms of the sectoral aid distribution. Since the dependent variable is the distribution of the aid sector, which is a continuous variable, I follow a linear regression strategy. However, the dependent variable is also bounded with 0 on the lower and 1 on the upper levels. To obtain a more unbiased estimate, I also employ Tobit analysis to uncover the relationship between the business-elite configuration and aid sector diversification. Table 5.7 demonstrates the results of OLS regression, and Table 5.8 demonstrates the results of Tobit analysis.

Table 5.7. OLS Analysis of Aid Sector Distribution

	Model 17	Model 18	Model 19	Model 20
Market Concentration	0.416*	0.449*	0.488*	0.229
	(1.97)	(2.13)	(2.30)	(1.04)
lnGDP_d	−0.0384***	−0.0463***	−0.0631***	−0.0605***
	(−10.14)	(−4.05)	(−5.07)	(−4.82)
lnGDP_r	−0.00386	0.0201***	0.0297***	0.0311***
	(−1.34)	(4.10)	(5.44)	(5.71)
lnPopulation_d		0.00576	0.0107	0.00848
		(0.83)	(1.46)	(1.15)
lnPopulation_r		−0.0294***	−0.0383***	−0.0400***
		(−5.99)	(−7.15)	(−7.43)
Contiguity			−0.0116	−0.0127
			(−1.38)	(−1.52)
Alliance			−0.0909***	−0.0945***
			(−5.76)	(−5.97)
OECD Membership_d				−0.00818
				(−0.16)
WTO Membership_d				−0.117***
				(−4.80)
WTO Membership_r				0.0118
				(0.91)
Cold War				0.00593
				(0.44)
Constant	1.908***	1.921***	2.227***	2.309***
	(13.61)	(8.81)	(9.32)	(9.59)
Observations	2,422	2,422	2,185	2,179
Adjusted R^2	0.052	0.066	0.080	0.088

t statistics in parentheses
*$p < 0.05$, **$p < 0.01$, ***$p < 0.001$

Table 5.8. Tobit Analysis of Aid Sector Fragmentation

	Model 21	Model 22	Model 23	Model 24
main				
Market Concentration	1.116*	1.249*	1.290*	0.229
	(2.21)	(2.45)	(2.53)	(1.04)
lnGDP_d	−0.0916***	−0.100***	−0.142***	−0.0605***
	(−9.92)	(−3.73)	(−4.82)	(−4.82)
lnGDP_r	−0.0121	0.0450***	0.0684***	0.0311***
	(−1.75)	(3.80)	(5.22)	(5.71)
lnPopulation_d		0.00828	0.0191	0.00848
		(0.50)	(1.10)	(1.15)
lnPopulation_r		−0.0699***	−0.0928***	−0.0400***
		(−5.89)	(−7.12)	(−7.43)
Contiguity			−0.0246	−0.0127
			(−1.23)	(−1.52)
Alliance			−0.230***	−0.0945***
			(−6.14)	(−5.97)
OECD Membership_d				−0.00818
				(−0.16)
WTO Membership_d				−0.117***
				(−4.80)
WTO Membership_r				0.0118
				(0.91)
Cold War				0.00593
				(0.44)
Constant	3.786***	3.635***	4.427***	2.309***
	(11.01)	(7.04)	(7.79)	(9.59)
/				
var(e.aidsectorindex)	0.278***	0.273***	0.267***	
	(19.22)	(19.23)	(18.31)	
Observations	2,422	2,422	2,185	2,179
Adjusted R^2				0.088

t statistics in parentheses
*$p < 0.05$, **$p < 0.01$, ***$p < 0.001$

Both OLS and Tobit analyses estimate the impact of the level of market concentration on the aid sector preferences of non-democratic donors. Model 17 in the OLS analysis uses the level of market concentration as the primary dependent variable and tests the relationship using only GDP control variables. The result of Model 17 shows that the more dominant market in the donor country is, in other words, the higher dominance in the business-elite configuration, the higher dominance in the sector of provided aid will be. The result is significant, although not at the level of $p < 0.01$. Even though this result seems robust with the control variables such as population, contiguity, and alliance, once I include the WTO, OECD membership, and the Cold War variables, the significance of the results disappears.

In the Tobit analysis, we see the same direction and similar tendency in the relationship between market concentration and aid sector distribution. Although the results are significant for the first three models, supporting the hypothesis, the significance disappears, similar to the OLS models.

As the third hypothesis, I test the third preference of the non-democratic and illiberal donors: the type of recipients. To test whether the level of competition in donors' market has an impact on the selection of the recipient, I benefit from two different statistical tests. The first one is linear regression because the dependent variable in the first hypothesis is the level of natural resources as a share of country's GDP. On the other hand, the second one is ologit estimation because the dependent variable is the income level group of the recipient country in the second hypothesis. Results of the analysis can be found in Tables 5.9 and 5.10.

Table 5.9. OLS Analysis of Type of Recipient

	Model 25	Model 26	Model 27	Model 28
Market Concentration	−4.715**	−5.210***	−5.133***	−4.096*
	(−2.91)	(−3.45)	(−3.35)	(−2.56)
lnGDP_d	0.112***	0.335***	0.386***	0.393***
	(3.84)	(4.09)	(4.28)	(4.31)
lnGDP_r	0.194***	−0.372***	−0.358***	−0.365***
	(8.66)	(−10.65)	(−9.15)	(−9.29)
lnPopulation_d		−0.158**	−0.185***	−0.189***
		(−3.17)	(−3.50)	(−3.54)
lnPopulation_r		0.715***	0.713***	0.716***
		(20.03)	(18.06)	(18.00)
Contiguity			0.0329	0.0376
			(0.55)	(0.63)
Alliance			−0.177	−0.172
			(−1.56)	(−1.51)
OECD Membership_d				0.0706
				(0.19)
WTO Membership_d				0.396*
				(2.26)

(Continued)

Table 5.9. Continued

	Model 25	Model 26	Model 27	Model 28
WTO Membership_r				0.0398
				(0.42)
Cold War				0.0411
				(0.42)
Constant	−6.005***	−7.324***	−8.489***	−8.980***
	(−5.52)	(−4.67)	(−4.89)	(−5.12)
Observations	2,379	2,379	2,145	2,139
Adjusted R^2	0.039	0.179	0.184	0.184

t statistics in parentheses
$*p < 0.05$, $**p < 0.01$, $***p < 0.001$

Table 5.9 demonstrates the results of whether non-democratic or illiberal governments with a high degree of concentration in their business-elite structure are more likely to provide assistance to the resource-rich countries as a result of the influence of the dominant business elite. The models in Table 5.9 use the log of total natural resources of recipients as a share of their GDP variable as the dependent variable. Model 25 provides the results only, including the GDP control variables. According to these results, as the level of concentration in the donors' business-elite configuration increases, they target the countries with lower natural resources as their recipients. Also, the results are robust with respect to the inclusion of the additional control variables in Model 26, Model 27, and Model 28. However, this finding is the contrary to what the original hypothesis suggests. Rather than resource-rich countries, countries with dominant elite structures provide aid to the relatively resource-scarce countries. Table 5.10 also shows the results of the analyses on the relationship between elite configuration and type of recipient by using the income group level of recipients as the dependent variable.

Table 5.10. Ordinal Logit Analysis of Type of Recipient

	Model 29	Model 30	Model 31	Model 32
recipient income code				
Market Concentration	−8.318***	−23.73***	−22.34***	−21.00***
	(−5.17)	(−8.44)	(−7.79)	(−7.09)
lnGDP_d	−0.0880**	0.839***	0.819***	0.845***
	(−3.17)	(6.04)	(5.35)	(5.41)
lnGDP_r	0.290***	5.547 ***	5.555***	5.592***
	(13.23)	(27.60)	(25.92)	(25.72)
lnPopulation_d		−0.630***	−0.609***	−0.621***
		(−7.27)	(−6.59)	(−6.60)
lnPopulation_r		−5.554***	−5.559***	−5.613***
		(−27.63)	(−25.99)	(−25.78)
Contiguity			0.125	0.132
			(1.37)	(1.42)
Alliance			−0.103	−0.0817
			(−0.59)	(0.46)
OECD Membership_d				0.446
				(0.73)
WTO Membership_d				0.831*
				(2.52)
WTO Membership_r				0.222
				(1.39)
Cold War				0.110
				(0.66)
/				
cut1	3.317**	49.20***	49.37***	50.95***
	(3.21)	(16.08)	(14.67)	(14.73)
cut2	5.027***	56.42***	56.58***	58.25***
	(4.85)	(17.59)	(16.09)	(16.11)
cut3	7.916***	64.19***	64.58***	66.33***
	(7.54)	(19.01)	(17.47)	(17.45)
Observations	2,434	2,434	2,196	2,190
Adjusted R^2				

t statistics in parentheses
*$p < 0.05$, **$p < 0.01$, ***$p < 0.001$

Furthermore, Table 5.10 represents the analysis between concentration in the elite structure and type of aid recipient and presents the results of the ordinal logit analysis with the recipient income group as the dependent variable. Similar to the OLS results with the recipients' natural resources variables, the findings, as a result of ordinal logit analysis, also show that non-democratic and illiberal donors with a high concentration in their business-elite structure are more likely to provide assistance to the lower-income group countries. Again, this is contrary to the hypothesis and will be discussed in a more detailed way in the conclusion chapter.

Although the result does not support the hypothesis in the expected direction, the relationship is significant even with respect to the inclusive of the additional variables in Model 30, Model 31, and Model 32.

As the last test, I re-test the relationship with the oprobit analysis in order to see if the results are robust with respect to different tests. The results of the ordinal probit analysis can be found in Table 5.11.

Table 5.11. Ordinal Probit Analysis of Type of Recipient

	Model 33	Model 34	Model 35
recipient income code			
Market Concentration	−4.619***	−4.211***	−3.493***
	(−4.96)	(−4.42)	(−3.51)
lnGDP_d	−0.0500**	0.00698	0.0106
	(−3.02)	(0.36)	(0.54)
lnGDP_r	0.165***	0.150***	0.155***
	(13.13)	(11.00)	(11.18)
Contiguity		0.0334	0.0390
		(0.93)	(1.08)
Alliance		0.751***	0.788***
		(11.38)	(11.82)
OECD Membership_d			−0.00355
			(−0.02)
WTO Membership_d			0.528***
			(4.52)
WTO Membership_r			−0.176**
			(−3.02)
Cold War			0.117
			(1.92)
/			
cut1	1.868**	3.284***	3.969***
	(3.05)	(4.78)	(5.63)
cut2	2.898***	4.364***	5.058***
	(4.73)	(6.34)	(7.15)
cut3	4.319***	5.853***	6.556***

Table 5.11.   Continued

	Model 33	Model 34	Model 35
	(7.00)	(8.43)	(9.19)
Observations	2,434	2,196	2,190
Pseudo R^2	0.039	0.070	0.076

t statistics in parentheses
$^*p < 0.05$, $^{**}p < 0.01$, $^{***}p < 0.001$

In agreement with the previous tests for the third hypothesis, the ordinal probit models also show that as the concentration in the donors' business-elite configuration increases, donor's prefer to provide assistance to the lower-income group countries. Including the additional control variables, the results still seem robust.

Chapter 6 Conclusion

Abstract: This chapter of the book discusses the findings of this study on the aid motivations and preferences of non-democratic or illiberal donors. In addition to the discussion of the findings, the chapter suggests theoretical and policy implications before concluding with the discussion on future research avenues regarding the motivations and preferences of non-democratic aid donors.

Keywords: Foreign Aid Policies, Non-Democratic Donors, Illiberal Donors, Non-DAC donors, Emerging Donors

6.1. Introduction

Peace and cooperation are often portrayed to be peculiar to a democratic or liberal state. This dominant argument and assumption are not specific to conflict, war, or alliance studies. Foreign assistance has recently become an attractive study area in terms of state cooperation, yet, providing foreign aid has also been characterized by the liberal characteristics of the government's policies. This common view appears to be undermined by recent foreign aid initiatives from non-democratic and/or illiberal regimes. South-south cooperation is one of the most significant examples of this recent development. Nonetheless, scholars have delved into the intention of non-democratic governments in giving foreign assistance and paid particular attention to the effectiveness of these countries' assistance.

In this book, I have developed a theory of foreign aid by non-democratic and illiberal countries concentrating on the motivation and preferences of foreign aid policies and testing the hypotheses of the theory empirically. The focus of the book has been the influence of export-oriented business elites on foreign aid policies. Following the literature review, chapter 3 has sketched a theoretical explanation of how non-democratic and illiberal governments provide foreign aid being influenced by the export-oriented business elites. The particular focus of the study has been the motivation and preferences of foreign aid policies. The empirical analyses have tested the theory and showed the influence of export-oriented businesses on not only providing foreign assistance but also on the value of the aid projects, selection of the recipients, and variation of the aid sectors.

6.2. Summary of the Findings

Relying on the suggested theory in chapter 3, this research has aimed to address four main hypotheses focusing on the two aspects of aid-giving: motivation and preferences. The first hypothesis tested the motivation, whereas the remaining hypotheses tested the preferences of non-democratic countries in aid giving.

Hypothesis 1: Autocratic and illiberal states with a high degree of political influence from the export-oriented business elite are more likely to provide foreign aid than the other autocratic and illiberal states.

The first hypothesis was tested with multiple dependent variables and tests. When run in logit regression with aid giving as the dependent variable, the measure of the political influence of export-oriented business elites was statistically significant. However, in none of the models, the results were significant at a higher level, such as .001. Although the measure is not highly significant at the level of .001, the statistical significance has not disappeared with different measures of political influence and aid motivation. For example, the hypothesis was also tested running in OLS regression with the aid amount variable. Nonetheless, the direction and statistical significance between the dependent and independent variables remained. The result remained statistically significant when combining two variables under the Heckman Selection model.

According to my theory, it was expected that there would be a relationship between the political influence of export-oriented business elites and non-democratic governments' aid-giving. As the results show, the more politically influential export-oriented business elites are, the higher the likelihood that a non-democratic or illiberal country provides foreign assistance and provides a higher amount of assistance.

However, are those politically influential export-oriented business elites necessarily and certainly involved with the aid projects? The Enterprise Survey provides general information about the firms but does not have specific information for the firms that are involved in the aid projects, or the study does not state whether these companies have benefited from these aid projects. Therefore, what we can infer from the results is limited to the conclusion that the higher the political influence in a non-democratic country in general, the higher the probability they might provide aid. Because, in non-democratic countries, the politically influential business elites are mostly within the supporting coalition of the government, we can infer that they are, in some ways, involved in the government's policies, including foreign aid policies. This is still supportive to my theory. On the other hand, to trace the involvement of business elites in aid policies, a future study can be implemented on the firms that are specifically involved in aid projects.

The reason why the results were *not highly significant but still consistently significant* across multiple models and variables might be related to the number of observations pertaining to the available data. The data of the measure of the independent variable is taken from the Enterprise Survey. Though Enterprise Survey is the most extensive dataset on firms in most authoritarian countries, data for Arab population donors such as Saudi Arabia is still missing. Also, although countries provide aid for multiple years, the Enterprise Survey provides limited information covering only one or two years regarding these countries. Including these missing cases in the analysis might strengthen the results.

The second hypothesis have focused on the preferences of non-democratic and illiberal governments in their aid policies, and the first preference has been identified as the value of the aid projects.

> *Hypothesis 2a: The less distribution in the configuration of the business elite, the higher number of projects with a higher amount of value will be provided by the autocratic and illiberal donors.*
>
> *Hypothesis 2b: The higher distribution in the configuration of the business elite, the higher number of aid projects with a lower amount of value will be provided from the autocratic and illiberal donors.*

The second group of hypotheses was tested with a couple of dependent variables and multiple models. In regard to these hypotheses, the results were significant, even including the control variables. Measures of concentration of business elites were positive and statistically significant on the number of high-amount aid projects. That being said, we can conclude that the configuration of export-oriented business elites in the country influences non-democratic or illiberal countries' preferences on the value of their projects.

Theoretically, given the influence of export-oriented business elites on non-democratic donors, I would expect the value of their aid projects to be determined based on the interests of export-oriented business elites. In this regard, the configuration of business elites is important. If there are certain dominant business elites within the supporting coalition of the leader, then higher-value of projects would benefit these business elites more. However, it is still a question whether these dominant export-oriented elites are within the supporting coalition of the leader in a country with autocratic or illiberal regime type. Although the data is not specifically from the members of the supporting coalition of the leader, studies on autocratic regimes agree that elites, including the business elites, are usually within the supporting coalition of the leader in autocratic countries.

In conjunction with the high-value projects, the competition in the business-elite configuration also increases the number of low-value projects. When there is a higher level of competition among the business elites, the leader in the non-democratic country does not rely on the specific dominant business elites for the maintenance of his rule. There is a challenge against his rule because any of these business elites might support the opposition candidates if their interests are not met. In order to keep these diverse business groups as his supporters, the leader needs to share the economic resources more equally among the members of this elite group. The value of the aid projects provided decreases as the budget for foreign assistance is shared among many different business elites. As a result, the decrease in concentration among the business elites causes an increase in the number of low-value projects.

The third hypothesis was also on the preference of foreign aid, but this hypothesis tested the sectoral distribution of non-democratic or illiberal donors' foreign assistance.

Hypothesis 3: The higher distribution in the configuration of the business elite, the more variation in the sector of aid provided by the autocratic or illiberal donor countries.

The data and analysis used for testing this hypothesis showed that the non-democratic or illiberal donor countries with higher dominance business-elite structure are more likely to show higher dominance in the sectoral distribution of their foreign assistance. The result was statistically significant in most of the models.

In line with the theory, when the business elites are highly concentrated, the leader of the country will provide aid based on the interest of this concentrated business elite. For example, if there is a dominance in the business elites, and this dominant business elite is in the sector of construction, aid projects might be heavily on construction, decreasing the diversification within the aid projects.

However, when adding the membership of international organizations control variables, the significant result disappeared, although it still remained in the same direction. This disappearance of statistical significance indicates that donors' and/or recipients' membership to international organizations, such as the WTO or OECD, affect both levels of competition among the business elites in the donor countries and the sectoral distribution of these countries' assistance.

In addition to the value and sectoral preferences of the aid policies, the fourth hypothesis was also on the preference of foreign aid and tested the donors' selection of the recipient country for the foreign aid. It tested the type of recipients with regard to recipients' income level.

Hypothesis 4: Autocratic and illiberal donors with a more dominant business-elite structure are more likely to target resource-rich and middle-income countries as their recipients.

The fourth hypothesis, however, shows some discrepancies with the theory. To be more specific, rather than supporting the hypothesis in the same direction, the results show the opposite direction in the relationship between the business-elite configuration and the type of recipients. On the other hand, the results are highly significant, even including the control variables. Based on that result, we can mainly reach two conclusions: First, there is a causal relationship between the configuration of business elites in the non-democratic donor country and the type of recipient country. Second, when the level of dominance among the business elites in the donor country increases, the donor government is more likely to select lower-income countries. In other words, when the level of competition between the business elites increases, the government is more likely to select higher-income countries as their recipients.

This result leaves us with some questions: why would a non-democratic or illiberal donor country with a high level of competition among its business elites provide aid to the lower-income countries than a non-democratic donor country with a dominant business-elite structure?

There might be a couple of convincing reasons why a non-democratic country with high competition among its business elites would provide more help to countries with higher income. First, when there is a high level of competition among business elites, this competition might be reflected in the type of recipients as the continuation of the competition between the elites. High-income or resource-rich countries can provide more trade opportunities for the competitive nature of the business-elite configuration. Since we already know that the business elites are influential in aid giving regardless of the level of competition, there should be the reflection of business-elite configuration, even in high-level competition. Second, when there is a high level of competition between the elites, the leader might be more responsive and amenable regarding the interests of the entire business-elite configuration (all the members in the configuration). If the recipient preferences of these business elites are in the higher-income countries, the leader is influenced by their preferences due to the tendency to keep the elites with him and prevent them from supporting the opposition. There might be more pressure from the business elites on the leader when there is a high level of diversification between the elites than when there is dominance on the elite configuration. As a result, the aid policies are targeted at resource-rich countries.

This is still a significant finding as it highlights that non-democracies or illiberal countries do not always target the resource-rich or high-income countries as their recipients. Moreover, their aid policies still, account for the altruistic motivations when there is a dominance in their business-elite configuration. When autocratic or illiberal countries have dominance in the business-elite structure, they are more likely to assist to lower-income countries. Even though business elite is influential on foreign aid policies, the dominance in the business-elite structure would lead the non-democratic governance to assist lower-income countries.

6.3. Significance of the Study

This study is theoretically or empirically significant for four major reasons. Majority of the significance comes from the contribution of the study in different fields of political science with regards to its scope, theory, and findings.

The main significance of this study comes from its theoretical contribution to the foreign aid literature. Although many scholars have studied the motivation of foreign assistance, non-democratic assistance is still an unknown area that calls for further research. Moreover, up to now, there is no extensive theory accounting for the foreign assistance of non-democratic countries. This study fills this gap and suggests a theory of non-democratic foreign assistance.

Another significance of this study, again, is related to its contribution to the politically influential or politically connected firms literature. Although arguments are made about the firms' involvements in the foreign aid projects, these involvements have usually been evaluated in a limited number of country-cases and focused on traditional donors such as the US. Offering an explanation on business elites' influence in the non-democratic setting, this study contributes to the firms and international relations literature. This study merges the literature of firms and foreign aid.

Moreover, this study is significant because it provides a complementary picture of the foreign aid policies of non-democratic donors. This study takes into account not only the motivation of non-democratic donors but also analyzes the preferences of non-democratic donors. This allows us to have a more complementary explanation on their aid policies and to trace the influence of business elites not only on giving aid but also to whom to give and in which sector to give aid.

Last but not least, the findings of this study can be seen as an important contribution to the foreign aid and cooperation literature. The intention behind the foreign assistance of non-democratic governments has been questioned. This study clarifies that the assistance of non-democratic countries changes based on the elites. In this regard, the non-democratic governments are not profoundly different from the democratic governments as it is also shown that democratic governments do not provide foreign aid solely for altruistic motivations.

6.4. Limitations

There are several limitations to this study, most related to the data availability in non-democratic countries. First of all, foreign aid information about non-democratic countries is limited. OECD and AidData provide information about the foreign assistance of non-democratic countries; however, they come with two issues. First, not all non-democratic countries report their foreign assistance to the OECD. As a result, OECD uses estimates for these countries' foreign assistance instead of precise data. Second, even if AidData provides more extensive project-level information, yet it mostly relies on OECD data, whereas OECD's information is also limited. If more transparency in these countries can be achieved with consistent reporting to the OECD, then the problem of data limitation can be solved.

In addition to the foreign assistance data, the lack of sufficient information about the businesses in non-democratic countries is another limitation with regard to the data. Even if the World Bank Enterprise Survey contributes to the solution of this limitation, the Enterprise Survey has only one or two data points for each country between the years of 2002–2017. This causes data loss for non-democratic countries. Moreover, it does not include Arab countries, which are also non-democratic countries. This limits the reliability of the measures.

Another limitation of this study is related to the measurement. I have used only one measure of the political influence of business elites and only one measure for the concentration of the business elites. This limits the robustness of the substantive results. Having other alternative measures of these important variables would be a more robust test of my theory. Furthermore, the variable for the political influence of business elites comes from the Enterprise Survey. Again, this limits the robustness of my substantive findings in that the problems associated with the Enterprise Survey dataset characterize this variable.

Besides, I have not included an in-depth qualitative analysis in this research. Although the findings show that business elites are influential on aid policies, the findings still do not show exactly why business elites are so influential on foreign aid provision in non-democratic countries. In order to examine the reasoning behind this, an in-depth case study focusing on the business elites in non-democratic countries is needed. An in-depth qualitative case analysis with a process tracing methodology on the decision-making process of a specific non-democratic country could also elucidate the interaction between politically connected business elites and governments on foreign aid policies.

6.5. Implications

6.5.1. Theoretical Implications

The findings of this study suggest that there is a causal link between the business elites and foreign aid policies in non-democratic and illiberal countries, both in terms of motivation and preferences on foreign aid. We can see the relationship in the results of the analyses throughout this study.

Another theoretical implication we can infer from the findings of this study is related to the theories of aid effectiveness. Since countries began to provide foreign assistance, many economic resources have been circulating worldwide. While millions of dollars are provided as assistance, scholars began to question the effectiveness of this assistance and found mixed results with regard to the aid effectiveness. Concurrently, scholars drew attention to the motivation and/ or the reasons behind aid giving because aid might not be effective enough if it was not given for the reasons to be effective at all. Although this study does not directly measure the aid effectiveness, we can still make some implications about whether it is given to be effective or not. The findings of this study suggest that non-democracies with a higher level of dominance in their business-elite structure are more likely to provide aid to the lower-income countries. These findings theoretically imply that these non-democratic countries are still helping the countries in need, particularly when they have dominant business groups. This implies that they might provide aid to make it effective on the recipient nation's economy.

Another theoretical implication is related to international cooperation and foreign aid literature. Since foreign assistance from emerging donors, particularly within the South-South cooperation, has attracted the attention of scholars, scholars have been comparing the aid of traditional donors with the aid of emerging donors, specifically with China. This study focuses only on non-traditional donors. Although this study does not make a comparison between traditional and non-traditional donors, relying on the literature on traditional donors and the findings of this study, we can still figure out theoretical implications regarding the differences between their assistance. In this context, non-democracies, which are all emerging donors, are not seen to be profoundly different from the traditional democratic liberal donors in terms of their aims in increasing their trade balance. Non-traditional or non-democratic donors in this study, like the traditional donors, take into account their economic interests, and in the meantime, still might target the lower-income countries as their recipients. The difference between traditional and non-traditional donors might be in the level of importance of business elites. In democratic donors, although business interests might be relevant, the leader needs to take into account the elections, so s/he needs public support. Therefore, the importance of the influence of business elites might be restricted by the importance of the public support for a leader.

In addition to the theoretical implications in the field of aid effectiveness and international cooperation, this study also carries theoretical implications on domestic politics, particularly on the relationship between business elites and regime type. The findings also have significant theoretical implications, showing how crucial foreign aid can be for the leader in order to receive support from its coalition groups. In other words, even though aid might be effective and helpful in the recipient nation, it is also a useful tool for the government to maintain its rule since it can provide a resource opportunity that can be exchanged between the government and its politically connected businesses. This might also explain why the business elites in non-democracies are not motivated toward a regime change in non-democratic regimes. As Acemoglu and Robinson (2006) argue, elites might not have strong preferences for democracy as much as citizens, given that even foreign assistance can be beneficial for these elites to increase their capital in non-democracies.

6.5.2. Policy Implications

Research on foreign aid has significant political economy and international relations implications. While much of the latest research has revolved around the balance between foreign assistance and its effectiveness on development areas, there is a growing body of research on the domestic motivations of foreign assistance since it might be related to the effectiveness of foreign aid.

The findings of this research can be helpful in suggesting effective foreign assistance policy. To improve aid effectiveness and promote more foreign assistance, a non-democratic government can restrict the political influence of business elites on policy-making over the effectiveness of the aid because altruistic motivations need to be a priority to take into account the aid effectiveness. Beyond that, international organizations can set some rules for the countries to eliminate the influence of business elites on foreign aid.

Besides, governments must continue helping out the nations in need even when there is competition between the elites, given that the results demonstrate that competition between the business elites does not bring more assistance to the nations in need. If the competitive business elites are influential over the governments in selecting the recipient nations, governments need to encourage and persuade the competitive businesses for providing assistance to the nations in need rather than higher-income recipients.

6.6. Conclusion and Future Research

The statistically significant relationship between the influence and configuration of business elites and international foreign assistance gives some insight into an important issue and paves the way for further research. As shown, domestic politics and business elites matter in international relations. When it comes to foreign assistance and its effectiveness, we still try to understand the conditions that might make it effective. We already know aid is not always effective, and it is not always provided to make it effective and helpful by the governments. We also know that foreign assistance has some international motivations and consequences. However, we still need to know more about foreign assistance's domestic motivations and consequences. This research emphasizes the role of business elites as an important domestic factor in foreign assistance policies.

One way to extend the analysis in this study is to increase the number of observations. As discussed, both in chapter 4 and the limitations section of this chapter, the Enterprise Survey has limited information regarding Arab donors. Once the Enterprise Survey increases the number of observations, there might be more data available with regard to the political influence in the non-democratic donor countries. Extending the dataset by including more observations and replicating the tests might provide more valid results in the relationship between the political influence of business elites and foreign aid policies.

Another way to extend the dataset is to include more measurements for the political influence of business elites. Although the perception of corruption is one way to measure it, it does not fully capture the political influence and is an indirect measure. There might not be a direct measure of political influence since we cannot be sure that the firms will be explicit and transparent in their connections to the governments when they are asked. However, survey research or survey experiment can be implemented on a donor country's firms to understand their connections with the governments. One example can be conducting a survey only to the firms involved in the aid projects. Although not for all of the countries, AidData has provided project-level data for China's foreign aid projects, which also provides information about the companies that implemented the foreign aid projects. Drawing the universe of observations from these companies, a survey analysis can be conducted on Chinese companies. This would be particularly useful not only for understanding the connection between the government and aid project contractors but also for understanding the causal process and the degree of connection between the business elites and the government.

Another research can be implemented by comparing the influence of business elites on aid policies in non-democratic countries with the influence of business elites in democratic countries. This study might be useful to understand how much their influence varies by changing the regime type and uncovering the differences between traditional and non-traditional donors.

Overall, future research should focus on the case studies that uncover the causal mechanism between politically connected business elites and non-democratic governments and expand the dataset by including more evidence on the politically connected firms in those countries.

Appendix A

A.1. Chinese Foreign Assistance

Below is the graph that demonstrates the increase in Chinese foreign assistance over time between the years of 2011 and 2015. The graph is created based on the OECD estimates on the People's Republic of China whereas the graph on Chinese foreign assistance in the introduction chapter (Figure A.1) is created based on the OECD data for Chinese Taipei.

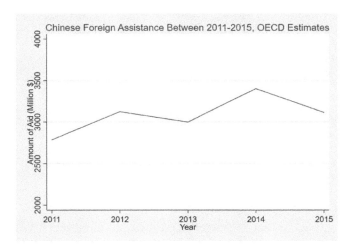

Figure A.1. Chinese Foreign Assistance Based on OECD Estimates

A.2. Country-Years Included in Analyses of Chapter 4

Below is the list of autocratic and illiberal countries between the years of 2002 and 2018 based on V-Dem's regime-type classification.

Table A.1. Country Observations in the Analyses of Chapter 4 (Years: 2002–2018)

Country List		
Afghanistan	Honduras	Philippines
Angola	Croatia	Papua New Guinea
United Arab Emirates	Hungary	Korea, Dem. People's Rep.
Argentina	Indonesia	Paraguay
Armenia	India	West Bank and Gaza
Azerbaijan	Iran, Islamic Rep.	Qatar
Burundi	Iraq	Romania
Burkina Faso	Jamaica	Russian Federation
Bangladesh	Jordan	Rwanda
Bulgaria	Kazakhstan	Saudi Arabia
Bahrain	Kenya	Sudan
Bosnia and Herzegovina	Kyrgyz Republic	Senegal
Belarus	Cambodia	Singapore
Bolivia	Kuwait	Solomon Islands
Brazil	Lao PDR	Sierra Leone
Barbados	Lebanon	El Salvador
Bhutan	Liberia	Somalia
Central African Republic	Libya	Serbia
China	Sri Lanka	South Sudan
Cameroon	Lesotho	Suriname
Congo, Dem. Rep.	Morocco	Slovak Republic
Congo, Rep.	Moldova	Seychelles
Colombia	Madagascar	Syrian Arab Republic
Comoros	Maldives	Chad
Cuba	Mexico	Togo
Djibouti	Macedonia, FYR	Thailand
Dominican Republic	Mali	Tajikistan
Algeria	Myanmar	Turkmenistan
Ecuador	Montenegro	Timor-Leste
Egypt, Arab Rep.	Mongolia	Tunisia
Eritrea	Mozambique	Turkey
Ethiopia	Mauritania	Tanzania

Table A.2. Continued

Country List		
Fiji	Malawi	Uganda
Gabon	Malaysia	Ukraine
Georgia	Namibia	Uzbekistan
Ghana	Niger	Venezuela, RB
Guinea	Nigeria	Vietnam
Gambia, The	Nicaragua	Vanuatu
Guinea-Bissau	Nepal	Kosovo
Equatorial Guinea	Oman	Yemen, Rep.
Guatemala	Pakistan	South Africa
Guyana	Panama	Zambia
Hong Kong SAR, China	Peru	Zimbabwe

Below is the list of autocratic and illiberal countries with years that have data point in Enterprise Survey (2019)

Table A.2. Countries in Enterprise Survey (2002–2018)

Years	Country
2008, 2014	Afghanistan
2006, 2010	Angola
2007	Albania
2006, 2010, 2017	Argentina
2009, 2013	Armenia
2009, 2013	Azerbaijan
2006, 2014	Burundi
2009	Benin
2009	Burkina Faso
2007, 2013	Bangladesh
2007, 2009, 2013	Bulgaria
2009, 2013	Bosnia and Herzegovina
2008, 2013	Belarus
2006, 2010, 2017	Bolivia
2009	Brazil
2010	Barbados

(*Continued*)

Table A.2. Continued

Years	Country
2009, 2015	Bhutan
2006, 2010	Botswana
2011	Central African Republic
2012	China
2009, 2016	Cameroon
2006, 2010, 2013	Congo, Dem. Rep.
2009	Congo, Rep.
2006, 2010, 2017	Colombia
2013	Djibouti
2010, 2016	Dominican Republic
2006,2010,2017	Ecuador
2013, 2016	Egypt, Arab Rep.
2009	Eritrea
2011, 2015	Ethiopia
2009	Fiji
2009	Gabon
2008, 2013	Georgia
2006, 2016	Guinea
2006	Gambia, The
2006	Guinea-Bissau
2006, 2010, 2017	Guatemala
2010	Guyana
2006, 2010, 2016	Honduras
2007, 2013	Croatia
2013	Hungary
2009, 2015	Indonesia
2014	India
2011	Iraq
2010	Jamaica
2013	Jordan
2009, 2013	Kazakhstan
2007, 2013	Kenya
2009, 2013	Kyrgyz Republic
2013, 2016	Cambodia
2009, 2012, 2016	Lao PDR
2013	Lebanon
2017	Liberia

Table A.2. Continued

Years	Country
2011	Sri Lanka
2009, 2016	Lesotho
2013	Morocco
2009, 2013	Moldova
2009, 2013	Madagascar
2006, 2010	Mexico
2009, 2013	Macedonia, FYR
2007, 2010,2 016	Mali
2014, 2016	Myanmar
2009, 2013	Montenegro
2009, 2013	Mongolia
2007	Mozambique
2006	Mauritania
2014	Mauritania
2009, 2014	Malawi
2015	Malaysia
2006, 2014	Namibia
2009, 2017	Niger
2007, 2014	Nigeria
2006, 2010, 2016	Nicaragua
2009, 2013	Nepal
2007, 2013	Pakistan
2006, 2010	Panama
2006, 2010, 2017	Peru
2009, 2015	Philippines
2015	Papua New Guinea
2006, 2010, 2017	Paraguay
2013	West Bank and Gaza
2009, 2013	Romania
2009, 2012	Russian Federation
2006, 2011	Rwanda
2014	Sudan
2007, 2014	Senegal
2015	Solomon Islands
2009, 2017	Sierra Leone

(*Continued*)

Table A.2.   Continued

Years	Country
2006, 2010, 2016	El Salvador
2009, 2013	Serbia
2014	South Sudan
2010	Suriname
2013	Slovak Republic
2009	Chad
2009, 2016	Togo
2016	Thailand
2008, 2013	Tajikistan
2009, 2015	Timor-Leste
2013	Tunisia
2008, 2013	Turkey
2006, 2013	Tanzania
2006, 2013	Uganda
2008, 2013	Ukraine
2008, 2013	Uzbekistan
2006, 2010	Venezuela, RB
2009, 2015	Vietnam
2009	Vanuatu
2009, 2013	Kosovo
2010, 2013	Yemen, Rep.
2007, 2013	Zambia
2011, 2016	Zimbabwe

A.3. Country-Years Included in Analyses of Chapter 5

Below is the list of autocratic and illiberal donors that are included in the analyses of chapter 5. The recipients are not included in the below list. However, the analyses have been implemented in dyad-year level.

Table A.3. Country and Years Used in Analyses of Chapter 5

Country	Years
Country	Years
Brazil	1998, 2001, 2004–2010
Chile	2002–2010
China	2000–2014
Columbia	2006–2010
Hungary	2006
India	2006–2010
Kuwait	1962–1968, 1970–2013
Qatar	2007
Romania	2007–2009
Saudi Arabia	1975–2011
Slovak Republic	2013
Taiwan	1990–2011
Thailand	2007–2010
United Arab Emirates	1972–1988, 1993, 1998–2013

Bibliography

Acemoglu, D., & Robinson, J. A. (2006). *Economic Origins of Dictatorship and Democracy.* Cambridge, UK: Cambridge University Press.

Acemoglu, D., Egorov, G., & Sonin, K. (2008). Coalition Formation in Non-Democracies. *The Review of Economic Studies,* 75(4), 987–1009, https://doi.org/10.1111/j.1467-937X.2008.00503.

AidData. (2017a). AidDataCore_ResearchRelease_Level1_v3.1. Williamsburg, VA: Aid-Data. Accessed on February 2, 2018. Retrieved from https://www.aiddata.org/data/aiddata-core-research-release-level-1-3-1.

AidData. (2017b). Chinese Global Official Finance Dataset, Version 1.0. Accessed on February 2, 2018. Retrieved from http://china.aiddata.org/downloads.

Alesina, A., & Dollar, D. (2000). Who Gives Foreign Aid to Whom and Why? *Journal of Economic Growth,* 5(1), 33–63.

Annen, K., & Strickland, S. (2017). Global Samaritans? Donor Election Cycles and the Allocation of Humanitarian Aid. *European Economic Review,* 96, 38–47. https://doi.org/10.1016/j.euroecorev.2017.04.006.

Apodaca, C. (2017). Foreign Aid as Foreign Policy Tool. Retrieved on January 30, 2018, from http://politics.oxfordre.com/view/10.1093/acrefore/9780190228637.001.0001/acrefore-9780190228637-e-332.

Asmus, G., Fuchs, A., & Muller, A. (2018). Russia's Foreign Aid Re-emerges. Accessed on June 5, 2019. Retrieved from https://www.aiddata.org/blog/russias-foreign-aid-reemerges.

Barthel, F., Neumayer, E., Nunnenkamp, P., & Selaya, P. (2014). Competition for Export Markets and the Allocation of Foreign Aid: The Role of Spatial Dependence among Donor Countries. *World Development,* 64, 350–365, https://doi.org/10.1016/j.worlddev.2014.06.009.

Bearce, D. H., & Tirone, D. C. (2010). Foreign Aid Effectiveness and the Strategic Goals of Donor Governments. *The Journal of Politics,* 72(3), 837–851. https://doi.org/10.1017/S0022381610000204.

Blaydes, L. (2008). *Competition without Democracy: Elections and Distributive Politics in Mubarak's Egypt.* Ph.D. thesis. University of California, Los Angeles.

Bluhm, R., Dreher, A., Fuchs, A., Parks, B., Strange, A., & Tierney, M. (2018). *Connective Financing: Chinese Infrastructure Projects and the Diffusion of Economic Activity in Developing Countries* (AidData Working Paper 64). Williamsburg, VA: AidData at William Mary.

Bratton, M. and N. Van de Walle (1997). *Democratic Experiments in Africa: Regime Transitions in Comparative perspective*. Cambridge: Cambridge University Press.

Brautigam, D. (2009). *The Dragon's Gift: The Real Story of China in Africa*. OUP Oxford.

Brautigam, D. (2011). Aid "With Chinese Characteristics": Chinese Foreign Aid and Development Finance Meet the OECD-DAC Aid Regime. *Journal of International Development*, 23(05), 752–764.

Breslin, S. (2013). China and the South: Objectives, Actors, and Interactions. *Development and Change*, 44(6), 1273–1294.

Browne, S. (2012). *Aid and Influence: Do Donors Help or Hinder?* Taylor Francis.

Cingranelli, D. L., Richards, D. L., & Clay, K. C. (2014). The CIRI Human Rights Dataset. http://www.humanrightsdata.com.

Clapham, C. S. (1985). *Third world politics: An introduction*. Univ of Wisconsin Press.

Coppedge, M., Gerring, J., Knutsen, C. H., Lindberg, S. I., Skaaning, S. E., Teorell, J., ... & Ziblatt, D. (2018a). V-Dem [Country-Year/Country-Date] Dataset v8 [Data set]. Varieties of Democracy (V-Dem) Project. https://www.v-dem.net/data/dataset-archive/country-year-v-dem-core-v8/

Coppedge, M., Gerring, J., Knutsen, C. H., Lindberg, S. I., Skaaning, S. E., Teorell, J., et al. (2018b). "V-Dem Codebook v8" Varieties of Democracy (V-Dem) Project. https://doi.org/10.23696/vdemcy18.

Correlates of War Project. (2013). Formal Alliances v4.1. http://www.correlatesofwar.org/data-sets/formal-alliances.

Correlates of War Project. (2016). Direct Contiguity Data, 1816–2016. Version 3.2. http://www.correlatesofwar.org/data-sets/direct-contiguity.

De Mesquita, B., Smith, A., Siverson, R. M., & Morrow, J. D. (2004). *The Logic of Political Survival* (Revised ed.). Cambridge, MA: The MIT Press.

De Mesquita, B. B., & Smith, A. (2007). Foreign Aid and Policy Concessions. *Journal of Conflict Resolution*, 51(2), 251–284. https://doi.org/10.1177/0022002706297696.

De Mesquita, B., & Smith, A. (2009). A Political Economy of Aid. *International Organization*, 63(2), 309–340. https://doi.org/10.1017/S0020818309090109.

De Mesquita, B. B., & Smith, A. (2012). Domestic Explanations of International Relations. *Annual Review of Political Science*, 15, 161–181.

Diven, P. J. (2001). The Domestic Determinants of US Food Aid Policy. *Food Policy*, 26, 455–474. https://doi.org/10.1016/S0306-9192(01)00006-9.

Dogan, M. (2003). *Elite Configurations at the Apex of Power*. Leiden/Boston: Brill.

Dreher, A., Nunnenkamp, P., & Thiele, R. (2011). Are 'New'Donors Different? Comparing the Allocation of Bilateral Aid Between nonDAC and DAC Donor Countries. *World Development*, 39(11), 1950–1968.

Dreher, A., & Fuchs, A. (2015). Rogue aid? An Empirical Analysis of China's Aid Allocation. *Canadian Journal of Economics*, 48(3), 988–1023.

Dreher, A., Fuchs, A., Parks, B., & Strange, A. M. (2017). *Aid, China, and Growth: Evidence from a New Global Development Finance Dataset* (AidData Working Paper TBD). Williamsburg, VA: AidData.

Enterprise Surveys. (2019). The World Bank. http://www.enterprisesurveys.org.

Frantz, E. (2018). *Authoritarianism: What Everyone Needs to Know*. New York: Oxford University Press.

Gandhi, J. (2008). *Political Institutions under Dictatorship*. Cambridge: Cambridge University Press. https://doi.org/10.1017/CBO9780511510090.

Gandhi, J., & Lust-Okar, E. (2009). Elections Under Authoritarianism. *Annual Review of Political Science*, 12. Available at SSRN: https://ssrn.com/abstract= 1445097.

Geddes, B. (1999). What do We Know about Democratization after 20 Years?. *Annual Review of Political Science*, 2, 115–144.

Geddes, B., Wright, J., & Frantz, E. (2018). *How Dictatorships Work: Power, Personalization, and Collapse*. Cambridge: Cambridge University Press. https://doi.org/10.1017/9781316336182.

Gibler, D. M. (2009). *International Military Alliances 1648–2008*. CQ Press.

Griffiths, J. (2017). Report Exposes Size of China's Secretive Aid Budget. Retrieved from http://www.cnn.com/2017/10/11/asia/china-overseas-aid/index.html.

Haas, M. l. (2003). Ideology and Alliances: British and French External Balancing Decisions in the 1930s. *Security Studies*, 12(4), 34–79. https://doi.org/10.1080/ 09636410390447626.

Hattori, T. (2001). Reconceptualizing Foreign Aid. *Review of International Political Economy*, 8(4), 633–660.

Higley, J., & Burton, M. (2006). *Elite Foundations of Liberal Democracy*. Oxford: Rowman Littlefield.

Kavakli, K. C. (2018). Domestic Politics and the Motives of Emerging Donors: Evidence from Turkish Foreign Aid. *Political Research Quarterly*, 71(3), 614–627. https://doi.org/10.1177/1065912917750783.

Kim, S. M. (2016). The Domestic Politics of International Developments in South Korea: Stakeholders and Competing Policy Discourses. *Pacific Review*, 29(1), 67–91.

Kuziemko, I., & Werker, E. (2006). How Much Is a Seat on the Security Council Worth? Foreign Aid and Bribery at the United Nations. *Journal of Political Economy*, 114(5), 905–930. https://doi.org/10.1086/507155.

Lai, B., & Morey, D. S. (2006). Impact of Regime Type on the Influence of U.S. Foreign Aid. *Foreign Policy Analysis*, 2(4), 385–404. https://doi.org/10.1111/j.1743-8594.2006.00037.x.

Lancaster, C. (2008). *Foreign Aid: Diplomacy, Development, Domestic Politics*. University of Chicago Press.

Levitsky, S., & Way, L. A. (2002). The Rise of Competitive Authoritarianism. *Journal of Democracy*, 13(2), 51–66.

Li, M. (2009). *Soft Power: China's Emerging Strategies in International Politics*. Lexington Books.

"List of OECD Member Countries-Ratification of the Convention on the OECD." OECD. Accessed February 3, 2019. Retrieved from http://www.oecd.org/about/membersandpartners/list-oecd-member-countries.htm.

Lumsdaine, D. H. (1987). *Ideals and Interests: The Foreign Aid Regime, 1949–1986*. Ph.D. thesis. California: Stanford University.

Lundsgaarde, E. (2013). *The Domestic Politics of Foreign Aid*. Routledge.

Marsot, A. G. (1969). China's Aid to Cambodia. *Pacific Affairs*, 42(2), 189–198.

Morgenthau, H. (1962). A Political Theory of Foreign Aid. *The American Political Science Review*, 56(2), 301–309. https://doi.org/10.2307/1952366.

Naim, M. (2009). Rogue Aid. *Foreign Policy*. Retrieved January 23, 2018, from https://foreignpolicy.com/2009/10/15/rogue-aid/.

Narizny, K. (2003). Both Guns and Butter, or Neither: Class Interests in the Political Economy of Rearmament. *The American Political Science Review*, 2, 203.

Nelson, J. M. (1968). Aid, Influence, and Foreign Policy. Retrieved from http://agris.fao.org/agris-search/search.do?recordID=US201300318049.

North, D., & Weingast, B. (1989). Constitutions and Commitment: The Evolution of Institutions Governing Public Choice in Seventeenth-Century England. *The Journal of Economic History*, 49(4), 803–832.

Nye, J. S. (1990). Soft Power. *Foreign Policy*, 80, 153–171. https://doi.org/10.2307/1148580.

OECD (2017), "Estimates of gross concessional flows for development co-operation, 2010–15: Million USD", in *Development Co-operation Report 2017: Data for Development*, OECD Publishing, Paris, https://doi.org/10.1787/dcr-2017-table395-en.

OECD. (2019a). OECD. Stat (Database). Retrieved February 25, 2019, from https://stats.oecd.org/Index.aspx.

OECD. (2019b). Net ODA (Indicator). Retrieved February 25, 2019. https://doi.org/10.1787/33346549-en.

OECD. (2019c). Gross National Income (Indicator). Retrieved February 25, 2019. https://doi.org/10.1787/8a36773a-en.

OECD. (2019d). QWIDS Query Wizard for International Development Statistics, OECD QWIDS. Retrieved February 6, 2019, from https://stats.oecd.org/qwids/.

OECD. (2019e). Member Countries. Retrieved February 6, 2019 from https://www.oecd.org/about/members-and-partners/.

OECD. (2023). Development Finance of Countries beyond the DAC. Retrieved May 31, 2023, from https://www.oecd.org/dac/dac-global-relations/non-dac-reporting.htm.

Omoruyi, L. O. (2017). *Contending Theories on Development Aid: Post-Cold War Evidence from Africa*. Routledge.

Ottaway, M. (2003). *Democracy Challenged: The Rise of Semi-Authoritarianism*. Washington, DC: Carnegie Endowment for International Peace.

Pemstein, D., Marquardt, K. L., Tzelgov, E., Wang, Y., Medzihorsky, J., Krusell, J., Miri, F., & von Römer, J. (2019). *The V-Dem Measurement Model: Latent Variable Analysis for Cross-National and Cross-Temporal Expert-Coded Data* (V-Dem Working Paper, No. 21, 4th ed.). University of Gothenburg/Varieties of Democracy Institute.

Rai, K. B. (1980). Foreign Aid and Voting in the UN General Assembly, 1967–1976. *Journal of Peace Research*, 17(3), 269–277. https://doi.org/10.1177/002234338001700307.

Raposo, P. A. (2013). *Japan's Foreign Aid to Africa: Angola and Mozambique Within the TICAD Process*. Routledge.

Rhoades, S. A. (1993) The Herfindahl-Hirschman Index. *Federal Reserve Bulletin*, 79, 188.

Riddell, R. (1987). *Foreign Aid Reconsidered*. Johns Hopkins University Press.

Riddell, R. C. (2007). *Does Foreign Aid Really Work?* Oxford: Oxford University Press.

Ruttan, V. W. (1996). *United States Development Assistance Policy: The Domestic Politics of Foreign Economic Aid*. Johns Hopkins University Press.

Schraeder, P. J., Hook, S. W., & Taylor, B. (1998). Clarifying the Foreign Aid Puzzle: A Comparison of American, Japanese, French, and Swedish Aid

Flows. *World Politics*, 50(2), 294–323. https://doi.org/10.1017/S004388710 0008121.

Shinn, D. (2019). China's Economic Impact on Africa. *Oxford Research Encyclopedia of Politics*. Retrieved 18 May. 2023, from https://oxfordre.com/ politics/view/10.1093/acrefore/9780190228637.001.0001/acrefore-978019 0228637-e-831.

Singer, J. D., & Small, M. (1966). Formal Alliances, 1815—1939: A Quantitative Description. *Journal of Peace Research*, 3(1), 1–31.

Smith, B. H. (2014). *More Than Altruism: The Politics of Private Foreign Aid*. Princeton University Press.

Stinnett, D. M., Tir, J., Schafer, P., Diehl, P. F., & Gochman, C. (2002). The Correlates of War Project Direct Contiguity Data, Version 3. *Conflict Management and Peace Science*, 19(2), 58–66.

Suwa-Eisenmann, A., & Verdier, T. (2007). Aid and Trade. CEPR Discussion Paper No. DP6465. Available at SSRN: https://ssrn.com/abstract=1138578.

Tajoli, L. (1999). The Impact of Tied Aid on Trade Flows between Donor and Recipient Countries. *Journal of International Trade and Economic Development*, 8(4), 373–388.

Thul, C. P. (2017, November 28). *Cambodian PM Leaves for China to Seek More Aid*. Reuters. Retrieved January 23, 2018, from https://www.reuters.com/arti cle/us-cambodiachina-politics/cambodian-pm-leaves-for-china-to-seek-more-aid-idUSKBN1DT0H3.

Thul, C. P. (2018, January 11). China Signs New Aid Agreements with Cambodia. Reuters. Retrieved January 23, 2018, from https://www.reuters.com/arti cle/us-cambodiachina/china-signs-new-aid-agreements-with-cambodia-idUSKBN1F00IJ.

Tierney, M. J., Nielson, D. L., Hawkins, D. J., Roberts, J. T., Findley, M. J., Powers, R. M., Parks, B., Wilson, S. E., & Hicks, R. L. (2011). More Dollars than Sense: Refining Our Knowledge of Development Finance Using AidData. *World Development*, 39(11), 1891–1906.

Tingley, D. (2010). Donors and Domestic Politics: Political Influences on Foreign Aid Effort. *The Quarterly Review of Economics and Finance*, 50(1), 40–49. https://doi.org/10.1016/j.qref.2009.10.003.

Veltmeyer, H., & Petras, J. (2005). Foreign Aid, Neoliberalism and US Imperialism (Ch. 13). In A. Saad-Filho & D. Johnston (Eds.), *Neoliberalism: A Critical Reader*. Ann Arbor: Pluto Press.

Wallerstein, I. (1974). *The Modern World-System I: Capitalist Agriculture and the Origins of the European World-Economy in the Sixteenth Century*. New York: Academic Press.

Waltz, K. N. (1996). International Politics is not Foreign Policy. *Security Studies*, 6(1), 54–57. https://doi.org/10.1080/09636419608429298.

Wang, T. Y. (1999). U.S. Foreign Aid and UN Voting: An Analysis of Important Issues. *International Studies Quarterly*, 43(1), 199–210.

Wittkopf, E. R. (1973). Foreign Aid and United Nations Votes: A Comparative Study. *The American Political Science Review*, 67(3), 868–888. https://doi.org/10.2307/1958630.

Woods, N. (2008). Whose Aid? Whose Influence? China, Emerging Donors and the Silent Revolution in Development Assistance. *International Affairs*, 84(6), 1205–1221.

The World Bank, World Development Indicators. (2018a). GDP Per Capita (Database). Accessed February 10, 2019. https://data.worldbank.org/indicator/NY.GDP.PCAP.CD

The World Bank, World Development Indicators. (2018b). Population (Database). Accessed February 10, 2019. https://data.worldbank.org/indicator/SP.POP.TOTL.

The World Bank, World Development Indicators. (2018c). GDP Growth (Database). Accessed February 10, 2019. https://data.worldbank.org/indicator/NY.GDP.MKTP.KD.ZG.

The World Bank, World Development Indicators. (2018d). Total Natural Resources (Database). Accessed February 10, 2019. https://data.worldbank.org/indicator/NY.GDP.TOTL.RT.ZS.

The World Bank. (2019a). World Bank Country and Lending Groups (Data). Accessed February 10, 2019. https://datahelpdesk.worldbank.org/knowledgebase/articles/906519-world-bank-country-and-lending-groups

The World Bank. (2019b). TCData 360. Herfindahl Hirchman Index. Accessed February 10, 2019. https://tcdata360.worldbank.org/indicators/hh.mkt?country=BRAINDICATOR=2370VIZ=LINE_CHARTYEARS=&indicator=2370&countries=BRA&viz=line_chart&years=1988,2015.

Wright, J. (2009). How Foreign Aid Can Foster Democratization in Authoritarian Regimes. *American Journal of Political Science*, 53(3), 552–571. https://doi.org/10.1111/j.1540-5907.2009.00386.x.

WTO. (2019). Members and Observers. Retrieved February 28, 2019, from https://www.wto.org/english/thewto_e/whatis_e/tif_e/org6_e.htm.

Yuichi, D. K., & Montinola, G. R. (2009). Does Foreign Aid Support Autocrats, Democrats, or Both? *The Journal of Politics*, 71(2), 704–718. https://doi.org/10.1017/S0022381609090550.

Zakaria, F. (1997). The Rise of Illiberal Democracy. *Foreign Affairs*, 76(6), 22–43. https://doi.org/10.2307/20048274.

Zuckerman, A. (1977). The Concept "Political Elite": Lessons from Mosca and Pareto. *The Journal of Politics*, 39(2), 324–344.

Milton Keynes UK
Ingram Content Group UK Ltd.
UKHW040329070923
428189UK00003B/28

9 783631 885413